Adorno's study of Alban Berg is a unique document. Itself now a part of music history, it is a personal account, by a pre-eminent philosopher and aesthetician, of the life and musical works of his mentor, friend, and composition teacher.

Beyond the analyses of individual pieces, the book explores the historical and cultural significance of Berg's music and its relationship to that of other nineteenth- and twentieth-century composers and to the larger issues of contemporary life.

Alban Berg

Alban Berg a few weeks before his death

Alban Berg
Master of the smallest link

THEODOR W. ADORNO

*Translated with
introduction and annotation by*
JULIANE BRAND *and*
CHRISTOPHER HAILEY

CAMBRIDGE
UNIVERSITY PRESS

CAMBRIDGE UNIVERSITY PRESS
Cambridge, New York, Melbourne, Madrid, Cape Town, Singapore,
São Paulo, Delhi, Dubai, Tokyo, Mexico City

Cambridge University Press
The Edinburgh Building, Cambridge CB2 8RU, UK

Published in the United States of America by
Cambridge University Press, New York

www.cambridge.org
Information on this title: www.cambridge.org/9780521338844

First published in 1991
First paperback edition 1994
Reprinted 1997

A catalogue record for this publication is available from the British Library

Library of Congress Cataloguing in Publication Data

Adorno, Theodor W., 1903–1969.
[Berg, der Meister des kleinsten Übergangs. English]
Alban Berg, master of the smallest link / Theodor W. Adorno:
translated with introduction and annotation by Juliane Brand and
Christopher Hailey.
p.   cm.
Translation of: Berg, der Meister des kleinsten Übergangs.
Includes bibliographical references and index.
ISBN 0-521-33016-5. – ISBN 0-521-33884-0 (pbk.)
1. Berg, Aiban, 1885–1935   Criticism and interpretation.
I. Brand, Juliane.   II. Hailey, Christopher.   III. Title.
ML410.B47A6313   1991
780′.92–dc20   90-20146 CIP MN

ISBN 978-0-521-33016-9 Hardback
ISBN 978-0-521-33884-4 Paperback

Contents

Translators' introduction

Theodor Adorno's study of Alban Berg is not a central work of his music-aesthetic oeuvre. It has neither the breadth of his Mahler and Wagner monographs, nor the didactic focus of his *Philosophy of Modern Music* and *Introduction to the Sociology of Music.* It is, instead, a personal document, consisting of reminiscences about a mentor who became a friend, and analyses of works with which the author had lived a lifetime. And yet, because this relationship was of such crucial importance to Adorno, these works so decisive in shaping his aesthetic precepts, *Alban Berg*, its modest scope notwithstanding, provides a key to understanding the philosopher and his thought – as well as offering a unique perspective on one of this century's most representative creative artists.

In many ways, *Alban Berg: Der Meister des kleinsten Übergangs*, published near the end of its author's life, is a reflection upon and testimonial to a fondly remembered starting point. For Adorno (1903–1969) that starting point was an encounter with the world of the so-called Second Viennese School that had crystallized around the teaching, music, and personality of Arnold Schoenberg. In a post-war era surfeited with "novelty," the works of Schoenberg seemed genuinely "new," an eruptive creative presence marking a crossroad one could ignore only at the peril of losing one's way into the future. Yet it was not Schoenberg with whom Adorno chose to study, but his student Alban Berg, a composer who struck Adorno as a synthesis between Schoenberg and Mahler, between the bracing "air of another planet" and the bittersweet ache of memory.

Adorno's fascination with Berg and with the potency of that intersection of sensibilities is paralleled by his fascination with the city with which Schoenberg, Mahler, and Berg were so intimately associated: Vienna. For many young Germans of the 1920s, the restless energy of the Weimar Republic served to suppress any lingering nostalgia for or identification with the discredited Wilhelmine era. Memory – from the snug recollections of childhood to the conscious cultivation of cultural inheritance – was clouded by emotions ranging from embarrassment and guilt to disgust.

Translators' introduction

Post-war Vienna was a world apart. Divested of its polyglot empire, its glory grown musty, this metropolis of just under two million was a helpless giant mired in the past. But it was a giant blessed with an ironic awareness of its despair. In that ironic awareness of contradictions – anticipated in the music of Mahler and ever present in the works of Berg – Adorno found a metaphor for the piquancy and ambivalence of memory, a signifier for one of the larger issues with which he wrestled his life long. Is it any wonder, then, that Adorno's personal allegiance went not to Schoenberg, who thrice left Vienna for Berlin, but to Alban Berg, who thrice declined the opportunity?

Adorno first met Berg in June 1924, during a festival of new music in Frankfurt-am-Main, at which the composer's *Wozzeck* excerpts were given their premiere. At that time the twenty-one-year-old Adorno, active as a music critic and completing a Ph.D. in philosophy, was undecided between academia and a career in music. Thanks to comfortable family circumstances the decision was not pressing, and Adorno was able to pursue composition and piano studies on the side.[1] In his first letter to Berg in February 1925, Adorno, who had been studying theory and composition with the Frankfurt composer Bernhard Sekles since 1919, explained that he had recently encountered "specific technical problems" that he wanted to address under Berg's tutelage. With Berg's encouragement, Adorno moved to Vienna in March of that year, for what were to be several months of private study.

The correspondence between Adorno and Berg begins in earnest during Berg's 1925 summer vacation, which he spent in the country; Adorno remained in Vienna for a few weeks before embarking on his own vacation and in the fall returning to Frankfurt. From Adorno's letters, which seem forcedly familiar in tone, it is apparent that the young German had readily acclimated himself to Vienna's cozy world of café rendezvous, gossip, and intrigue. He embraces with alacrity the local household gods Peter Altenberg and Karl Kraus, and scatters reverential allusions to such perennial favorites of the Schoenberg circle as Strindberg and Wedekind. In curious counterpoint with these vestiges of Vienna's pre-war intellectual ambience are Adorno's up-to-the-minute situation reports on the pitched music-aesthetic campaigns of the post-war era, many of which were directed from the offices of Vienna's own new-music publisher, Universal Edition.

---

1 Adorno was the only child of the successful Frankfurt-am-Main wine merchant, Oskar Wiesengrund, a German Jew converted to Protestantism, and his Catholic wife, the singer Maria Cavelli-Adorno della Piana, the daughter of a German singer and a French-Corsican military officer of aristocratic lineage.

Translators' introduction

Founded in 1901, Universal Edition had become a major force in new music when its director, Emil Hertzka, offered exclusive contracts to Gustav Mahler, Franz Schreker, and Arnold Schoenberg in 1909. A decade later, with dozens of important composers under contract, Universal launched a prestigious journal, *Musikblätter des Anbruch* (later known simply as *Anbruch*), to publicize and propagate its catalogue of works. Adorno had been in Vienna scarcely three months when the director of Universal's opera division, Hans Heinsheimer, suggested he assume the editorship of *Anbruch*. Hertzka rejected the idea, but three years later the offer was renewed and, without leaving Frankfurt, Adorno served as an associate editor of *Anbruch* from 1928 to 1931.

Adorno had been writing about music since 1921, first in a Frankfurt literary review, then, beginning in 1923, as a Frankfurt correspondent for the arch-conservative Leipzig *Zeitschrift für Musik*, and, as of 1925, for the mainstream Berlin journal *Die Musik*. While the subject matter of his music criticism ranged from concert reviews to publication notices, its focus was contemporary music. From the outset he had demonstrated a particular empathy with the works of Schoenberg and his circle, and it is not surprising that close contact with members of that circle after 1925 should affect the tone and content of his writing.

One of the first products of that closer association was an *Anbruch* essay Adorno wrote for the 1925 Berlin premiere of Berg's *Wozzeck*.[2] It is an article that already articulates key elements of Adorno's Berg interpretation, including emphasis on the composer's proclivity toward "particle-like motivic material" and "symphonic extensivity" [*Extensität*], his all-consuming preoccupation with continual transformation, his critical embrace of the past, and the tension between subjective expression and objective formal control that positions Berg's music between that of Mahler and Schoenberg. What is more, the 1925 *Wozzeck* essay marked a turning point in the evolution of Adorno's writing style. In a 23 November 1925 letter to Berg, he describes his satisfaction with the essay, in which the logic of his argument does not pursue a string of surface associations but reflects through an intellectual continuum the simultaneity and factual parity of Berg's compositional intentions. Citing Berg's own dictum that for musical analysis to be adequate to its object it must employ a "compositional mode of expression,"[3] Adorno indicates that the very nature of his language and

2 "Alban Berg. Zur Uraufführung des *Wozzeck*," *Anbruch* VII/10 (December 1925), 531–537.
3 "Warum ist Schönbergs Musik so schwer verständlich," *Anbruch* VI/8 (August/September 1924), 329–341.

argument is inspired by the expressive characteristics and inner logic of musical composition. More specifically, Adorno notes a "curious intersection" between his intellectual development and Berg's compositional procedure, confiding that it is his secret desire to develop a prose equivalent to the manner in which Berg had composed his Op. 3 String Quartet. Adorno returned often to this "intersection" of verbal and musical syntax, as in a 16 January 1931 letter to Berg, in which he describes his recently completed Kierkegaard study (*Kierkegaard: Konstruktion des Ästhetischen*) as a work deeply indebted to "our" music. With obvious relish he adds that his new book was the object of many of the same criticisms levelled at the music of the Schoenberg circle, including disjointedness, unintelligibility, and overintellectualism.

Unfortunately, Adorno's eagerness to associate his paratactic prose style with the "musical prose" of the Schoenberg circle was not always considered flattering by the objects of the comparison. Both Schoenberg and Webern expressed dismay at the convolutions of Adorno's thought, and even Berg was bemused by his student's labyrinthine locutions. Characteristic is the anecdote told by Willi Reich about an Adorno lecture he and Berg listened to on the radio, during which the transmission was briefly interrupted. "What a shame we missed that passage," Berg observed, "it was no doubt the only straightforward sentence in the entire talk."[4]

Adorno maintained – with typically Schoenbergian aplomb – that the difficulty of his style reflected the complexity of intellectual material whose guiding principle was not ingratiating effect, but truth. Yet, even given the subtleties and layered intricacies of Adorno's thought, there is an unmistakable element of willful obfuscation in his sometimes rebarbative style. His delight in creative wordplay, arcane allusions, and logical elisions reflects not only the whimsy of an agile mind, but a decided ambivalence toward his readers. This is confirmed by a letter to Berg of 24 October 1926, in which he offers to write an introductory essay for the forthcoming production of *Wozzeck* in the Soviet Union. Anticipating Berg's qualms, he assures him that for proletarian readers he is capable of writing in a clear and straightforward style, something he found impossible to do for the bourgeoisie.

Adorno was a skilled composer and sophisticated analyst, but he never made his living as a musician, and, for all his intimate knowledge of the craft of composition, he remained an observer, more critical receptor than

4 Rosemary Hilmar Moravec recounts this incident, as told to her by Willi Reich, in her article, "Dr. Adorno war nur ein Schüler von Alban Berg," *Adorno in seinen musikalischen Schriften*, Musik im Diskurs, Volume II (Regensburg: Gustav Bosse Verlag, 1987), 107–137.

active participant. Something of that same "outsider" quality also characterized his relationship with the Schoenberg circle. When he arrived in Vienna in 1925 he was disappointed to find that circle not as cohesive as he had imagined, and, despite his inclination to speak about "our" music, his compositions received scant attention from his *compagnons d'armes*. And yet this oddly matched relationship between a precocious German philosopher and a loosely knit clique of Austrian musical revolutionaries a generation his senior was truly symbiotic. Beyond influencing the *style* of his writing, Adorno's compositional training and personal acquaintance with Berg, Webern, Schoenberg, and other major artistic personalities, gave the *content* of that writing an urgency and immediacy unmatched in the works of any other twentieth-century aesthetic philosopher. As a self-styled intellectual publicist for the "Second Viennese School," Adorno could speak with authority on technical matters, while at the same time abstracting from them philosophical insights which secured for this music a place of privilege for the intellectual elite of the inter- and post-war years.

It would be a gross oversimplification to reduce Adorno to a mere mouthpiece for Schoenberg and his circle, for the same technical expertise that afforded him insight into their works provided him with the criteria necessary for an independent aesthetic judgment. Adorno's misgivings about the emotional sterility of Schoenberg's early twelve-tone music, for instance, are documented in his letters and many of his later writings, including the present study. Specifically, as he wrote in a letter to Berg of 19 August 1926, Adorno was concerned that the twelve-tone technique, in which the row assures the derivation of each successive note, might prematurely abort the process of "imaginative hearing" and thereby eliminate the arbitrary, even inconsequent, decisions that are an essential element of the artist's freedom − the same freedom that Adorno reserved for himself in his writing. It is this freedom that Adorno finds preserved by Berg in such instances as the aesthetically problematic integration of a Carinthian folk song into his Violin Concerto or the clearly tonal references throughout his oeuvre. For Adorno, Berg's loyalty to the aesthetic sovereignty of "free atonality," coupled with his willingness to submit to the constraints of the twelve-tone technique, makes him a paradigm for the twentieth-century composer.

Of course Adorno's devotion to Berg went far beyond aesthetic affinity to a profound personal loyalty. He was proud that his teacher solicited his advice, going so far as to reproduce in his Berg book a facsimile of a letter in which the composer had asked his opinion about the relative merits of Wedekind's Lulu plays and Hauptmann's *Und Pippa tanzt* as subjects for his second opera. Conversely, in 1928, he seems genuinely aggrieved when it appeared that Paul von Klenau and not he had convinced Berg to publish the Seven Early Songs. (Adorno's enthusiasm for these works – in those years he ranked them with Schoenberg's Op. 6 songs – is curious in light of the apologetic tone he adopts in the present study.)

It may well be that Adorno overstates the closeness of his friendship to Berg. While he apparently served as a kind of courier during Berg's affair with Hanna Fuchs-Robettin, he was not the only student to abet Berg in his extra-marital dalliances.[5] Berg never offered Adorno the familiar "Du," and after 1925 the relationship was increasingly relegated to correspondence and occasional meetings, both of which became sporadic in the last years of Berg's life. There can be no doubt, however, of Berg's enormous respect for Adorno's accomplishments, both as a theoretician and composer. In a 1926 letter Berg wrote to his student:

I have become absolutely convinced that you are qualified to achieve the *highest* by way of profound insight into music (in all its as yet unexplored facets, be they philosophical, art historical, theoretical, social, historical, etc., etc. in nature) and will do so through major philosophical works. Whether in the process your musical works (I mean your compositions), upon which I have set such high hopes, are neglected, is a fear I always have when I think of you. It is clear: being that you are driven toward all or nothing (thank God!), you will one day have to choose Kant *or* Beethoven.[6]

Adorno was deeply shaken by Berg's untimely death in 1935. According to a letter to Helene Berg of 16 April 1936, his principal consolation lay in being able to propagate Berg's works through his writing, an activity that included the chapters contributed to Willi Reich's 1937 Berg biography, which form the basis for the present study. The authority of these chapters rests with the fact that Adorno had consulted closely with Berg on virtually all of his analytical articles; what he wrote after the composer's death clearly builds upon this foundation. As a result, the essays in the present study, though written over a span of thirty years, can be said to represent a sanctioned, if not exclusive, interpretation of the composer's works.

---

5 It is a tribute to Adorno's discretion that he never publicly betrayed the secret of Berg's affair with Hanna Fuchs-Robettin – save for the veiled allusions in his discussion of the *Lyric Suite*. His tactlessness, on the other hand, in rationalizing in a 1936 letter to Helene Berg both the affair and his role as intermediary displays a degree of insensitivity that amply explains her later reserve toward him. While she helped underwrite the publication of his Berg book, she declined to provide him with a preface he had requested and generously offered to outline for her.

6 Quoted in the afterword to *Theodor W. Adorno Gesammelte Schriften 19*/Musikalische Schriften, Volume VI, eds. Rolf Tiedemann and Klaus Schultz (Frankfurt-am-Main: Suhrkamp Verlag, 1984), 635.

Translators' introduction

In his chapter "Analysis and Berg," Adorno gives an elegant and compelling apologia of the purposes and goals of musical analysis. The hallmark of Adorno's own analyses is his uncanny ability to formulate through metaphor and analogy the essence of a work's inner dynamic. Moreover, he goes beyond the descriptive generalities of thematic analysis with detailed illustration of compositional process. And yet, as Diether de la Motte has noted, there is occasionally a discrepancy between Adorno's brilliant grasp of the whole − be it a single opus or an entire oeuvre − and his sometimes uninspired, even inaccurate discussions of specific musical details.[7] De la Motte surmises that Adorno's analyses were primarily inspired by what he *heard* and not by careful study of the score, which he seems to have found tedious. This seems plausible, for it would be fitting that as an analyst Adorno placed the same faith in "imaginative hearing" that he found so essential for the composer. As de la Motte concludes:

Perhaps he who can hear music in this way and comes thus to love it, he who understands music in this way and can call it by name but is a failure with the score, represents a disappearing type of dilettante who once made such essential contributions to musical culture and whose disappearance we should bitterly lament. The dilettante, who precisely because of his passionate love also always invests the same engagement in passionate hate.

In its passion, in the immediacy of its author's identification with his subject, Adorno's Berg study is unlike anything else he ever wrote on music. That same passion and identification account for the limitations of the book, which can serve neither as a factual biography, nor as an introductory guide to Berg's works. It is not an objective music historical account because it *is* music history, echoing both in Adorno's fierce loyalties as well as in his disdain for figures such as Stravinsky and Hindemith and denunciations of "New Objectivity" and "Neoclassicism" battles that once raged across the landscape of contemporary music. Ironically, it was his dissatisfaction with the burgeoning literature on the Second Viennese School, and in particular the Berg biography of Hans Ferdinand Redlich,[8] that galvanized Adorno into publishing his own Berg monograph. Thus, the present volume was intended from the outset as a corrective, as a means of resisting the tendency to allow Alban Berg to slip into history, of keeping memory vital.

---

7 Diether de la Motte, "Adornos musikalische Analysen," *Adorno und die Musik*, ed. Otto Kolleritsch (Graz: Universal Edition, 1979), 52–63.
8 Hans Ferdinand Redlich, *Alban Berg: Versuch einer Würdigung* (Vienna: Universal Edition, 1957).

A note on the translation

Translating Adorno is a notoriously daunting task. His use of language is brilliant and idiosyncratic, drawing liberally upon a knowledge of French, English, Latin, and Greek to infuse each word with radical meaning. His argumentation is a curious mixture of close reasoning and intuitive insight, critical perspicacity and capricious self-indulgence. At times one wishes he had had the services of a ruthless editor, and, as translator, one is tempted to intervene in ways ranging from breaking up sentences and paragraphs to searching for a more straightforward vocabulary. On the whole, we have resisted the temptation, in part so as not to misrepresent the *difficulty* of Adorno's prose – which he intended – and in part because his Berg study, though containing its fair share of puzzles, is not among his most recondite books. Indeed, its warm personal tone lends it an almost lyrical quality, especially in the passages of reminiscence.

Adorno is generally quite precise in his terminology. Therefore, context permitting, we have tried to be consistent in our translation of key terms, such as *Modell* (paradigm), *Rest* (remnant), *retten* (to salvage), and *Vermittlung* (mediation). Translating such key words is not always easy, and one of the most vexing terms appears in the very title of the book, *Meister des kleinsten Übergangs*. While one might normally translate *Übergang* as "transition", we felt that this word, with its emphasis on process, missed the essentially neutral quality of what Adorno sees as the Bergian *Übergang*, which need be no more than a single tone. Hence, we have chosen "link," which can refer backward or forward and yet remain a discrete entity. Another example is *Charakter*, which, following Schoenberg, Adorno uses to denote a distinctive musical idea, whether rhythmic, harmonic, melodic, timbral, or a combination thereof. As *Charakter* derives its extended meaning from *Charakterstück*, or *character piece*, we felt it reasonable to expect English readers to accept the same extension of meaning with "character." Realizing that no translation can give all shadings of meaning, the German original of these and other key terms appear in square brackets at their first appearance in the body of the text.

A note on the translation

Adorno did not intend access to his books to be easy and in consequence disliked indices, which offer the promise of particulate bits of available information. Berg, on the other hand, to paraphrase Adorno, was well-disposed toward indexing (having indulged his own penchant for pedantry by preparing one for Schoenberg's 1911 *Harmonielehre*) and it is in deference to him – as well as to the importance of Adorno's study as an historical source – that we have readily ignored Adorno's misgivings. Furthermore, we have used the index to give brief identification of individuals mentioned in the text, though we have refrained from adding explanatory footnotes. George Perle once recalled his first meeting with Adorno, during which the philosopher played for him on the piano without, it seemed, once taking his foot off the damper pedal. The effect of reading Adorno's prose is not dissimilar. Adorno seldom gives exact dates, is often vague about factual matters, and coy about his references and allusions. While such matters warrant clarification, a preoccupation with detail can interrupt the flow of his prose and blur the overall impression. Therefore, we have relegated all annotation material to an afterword, which the reader is free to consult or ignore. The most important additions therein are derived from earlier versions of the second chapter, "Reminiscence." Finally, there are instances in which the details of Adorno's musical analyses are confusing or inaccurate. Corrections or measure numbers added for clarification are given in square brackets.

Acknowledgments

We are grateful to Inge and Gerhard Brand, Mark De Voto, Michael Friedmann, Douglas Jarman, Martin Jay, Robert Morgan, and Janet Schmalfeldt for reading portions of the manuscript and giving valuable advice. Special thanks go to Rosemary Moravec and other members of the staff of the Österreichische Nationalbibliothek in Vienna for their assistance in locating relevant background material. Most important is our gratitude to Penny Souster, a good friend and patient editor.

Music examples are reproduced by permission of Universal Edition, Vienna.

Preface

The *captatio benevolentiae*, that an author hesitated taking up a suggestion to publish a book, is the worse for wear from persistent misuse. Usually it is invoked merely to relieve the author of responsibility. In the case of this book on Berg, however, it not only reflects the actual situation, but is crucial to an explanation thereof.

Elisabeth Lafite's kind invitation that the author, using earlier material, write a Berg monograph for the series "Österreichische Komponisten des XX. Jahrhunderts," aroused misgivings on two counts. First, he feared repeating himself, having published a great deal on Berg in the course of the forty years since coming to Vienna as Berg's student. He tried to avoid that insofar as possible, but could not eliminate all duplication between the chapter "Reminiscence" and the essay in *Klangfiguren*. Only texts that do not appear in the author's other books are incorporated into this volume.

In the meantime compendious works on the composer have been published. That raised the question whether a monograph might not be superfluous.

However, consideration of these, the author's own objections, led to his decision to accept the invitation. The bulk of his work on Berg consisted of the analyses and reflections he had contributed to the book published by Willi Reich in 1937, which was meant to be a preliminary study only. That book has long been out of print. The author deems those contributions, which in his opinion stemmed from a period of breakthrough, worthy of being made available again to the public. He thanks Willi Reich for his generous permission. Of course, the author considers what he wrote for this book in 1968 its most significant portion.

It may be above all several of the more recent publications that legitimize the book. If musicologists who once sought to neutralize Schoenberg historically as a "great isolated figure" and thus intern him in a kind of spiritual solitary confinement, if musicologists who during the years of political darkness prided themselves on their identification with folk music – if these people now begin reaching out toward Berg – then for this

Preface

author it is nothing but an attempt retroactively to extend the monopoly of their academic discipline to that sphere where decades ago they feared being compromised. The author's sympathy with that way of thinking is in inverse proportion to his hopes that the book may speak to those younger musicologists who are of a different stamp. Specifically, he would more than welcome a comparison of the chapters published in 1937 with the work of H. F. Redlich. He does not intend to praise, but rather, as a musician of the Second Viennese School, from which he never strayed, to share experiences relating to the person and oeuvre of Berg. In so doing a new concept of analysis emerged; in no way does he claim with what is presented here to have fulfilled the requirements of that concept. Nor are differences between the old and the new in any way smoothed over. The fact that the book itself documents a development is not incompatible with its subject.

On the occasion of a longer separation Alban Berg wrote the author a postcard quoting Hagen's passage from *Götterdämmerung*: "Sei treu" ("Be true"). It is the author's dearest wish not to have fallen short of that – without, however, allowing his passionate gratitude to encroach upon the autonomy his teacher and friend developed musically within him.

Frankfurt, September 1968

Tone

Familiar from childhood is the last movement of Haydn's "Farewell" Symphony, that F# minor piece in which one instrument after another ceases to play and departs, until finally only two violins remain to extinguish the light. Above and beyond the work's innocuous motivation and that sphere which repellant familiarity equates with Papa Haydn's sense of humor is the intent to compose farewell, to fashion the vanishing of music and to realize a potential that for those who penetrate its mystery has ever lurked in the very evanescence of musical material. Looking back on the works of Alban Berg, who, if alive today, would be over eighty years old, it seems as though his entire oeuvre was directed toward surpassing Haydn's flash of inspiration, toward reshaping music itself into a metaphor of vanishing, and with music to say adieu to life. Complicity with death, an urbane cordiality toward his own extinction, are characteristics of his work. Only those who understand Alban Berg's music as a product of these characteristics, and not as a matter of historical style, can truly experience it. One of his most mature and perfect compositions, the *Lyric Suite* for string quartet, closes without closing, open-ended, without a final barline and with only a major third motive in the viola, which according to the composer's directive may be repeated *ad libitum* several times until becoming quite inaudible. This profoundly melancholy dissolution of the music, which is granted no affirming finality, sounds as though what in Haydn still seemed harmless play had here taken on the gravity of desolate, open infinity. But it also bears a trace of that hope which music at its Bachian heights once infused into the chorales accompanying mortals through a gateway into darkness so complete as to be capable of kindling the final light. It would be foolish to interpret the inclusion of the chorale "Es ist genug" from the cantata "O Ewigkeit, du Donnerwort" in the Violin Concerto as mere poetic design or even as a concession to a formula of reconciliation. Had Berg been content with that, he could have had an easier time of it; he need not have grafted a foreign element on to his finale and left it there so conspicuously as to be more shocking than almost any

1

Alban Berg

dissonance. Rather, with this quotation, whose stylistic recklessness would least of all have escaped Berg's own refined awareness, it is as if he had wearied of all the rounded forms and aesthetic internalization on which he had lavished his life; as if, directly, impatiently, he wanted to make sure to say in the last minute, indeed, to call by name — as a protest against art itself — that nameless thing around which his art was organized. Evanescence, the revocation of one's own existence, is for Berg not the stuff of expression, not music's allegorical theme, but rather the law to which music submits. Symphonic composers like Berg, composers of the large forms, are often credited with knowing how to construct their edifices with the smallest building blocks, as if out of nothing. Certainly there is a rule of proportion for large forms that makes closure and coherence dependent upon the fact that no single element within it asserts an individual identity independent of the whole. In Berg the atomization of the material and the integration granted it are, without question, in mutual accord. But in his case such atomization has an underlying motivation. Those minuscule motives, which drew nitpicking scorn from the Beckmessers during Berg's lifetime, do not really possess the ambition to establish themselves and unite into a massive and powerful whole. In immersing oneself in Berg's music one feels at times as though Berg's voice were speaking in a tone combining gentleness, nihilism, and intimate trust to the point of utter enervation: "Oh well, in the end, it's all really nothing." Under an analytic gaze this music completely dissolves, as if it contained no solid components. It vanishes even while still in its apparently fixed, objectified aggregate state. Had one drawn Berg's attention to this he would, in his own bashful way, have been as pleased as someone caught in a secret kindness. The ramified, organically luxuriant richness of many of his creations, as well as the disciplining skill to bind together the diffuse and divergent — a skill reminiscent of childish, painstakingly executed drawing-board pictures — proves at heart to be simpy a means of emphasizing the idea that all is nothing through the contrast inherent in erecting an elaborate musical structure that springs from nothingness and trickles away into nothingness. If these works expand the process of the "Farewell" Symphony to disproportionate dimensions, they are nonetheless faithful to an Austrian tradition: the note of resignation discovered by Schubert, but also the folk-like quality of Raimund's dialect, with its simultaneously foolish and wise combination of skepticism and catholicity, in *Der Bauer als Millionär* and Valentin in *Der Verschwender*. For all the austere refinement of its compositional technique, Berg's music speaks in dialect. The performance indication "wienerisch" given a theme in the Violin Concerto — anything but a superimposition of folkloric seasoning — admits as much. And yet it is this nonchalantly ingratiating

2

Viennese theme that then gives rise to the deadly quality that undermines the *Ländler*.

In musical material nothingness has its equivalent in the half-step that extends barely beyond the tone itself, yet establishes no melodic profile of its own – still this side of the plasticity of intervals and therefore ever ready to fall back into amorphousness. Berg, probably alone among the masters of new music, was a chromaticist through and through; at their core most of his themes can be reduced to half-steps, and that is why these themes never acquire the firm, set character befitting traditional symphonic music. Of course Berg's music, with its eminent instinct for continuity and articulation, does not exhaust itself in a monotony of chromaticism, as does for instance Reger's. Rather, Berg's compositional niveau proves itself – on a level so high that it is scarcely even perceived today – precisely in that extremely deliberate syntactical organization, which extends from the movement as a whole to the proper position of every single note, omitting nothing. This music is beautiful in the sense of the Latin concept *formosus*, the concept of the richness of forms. Its formal wealth imbues it with eloquence and with an inherent similarity to language. But Berg possesses a special technique for taking defined thematic shapes and, in the course of developing them, calling them back to nothingness. Wagner, who was the first to compose essentially chromatically, defined composition as the art of transition. Already with him chromaticism, a means for creating an imperceptible flow of events, served – at least in *Tristan* – to turn music altogether into transition, transformation, seamless self-transcendence. From that Berg developed a stylistic manner he pursued almost to the point of idiosyncrasy. He fused the art of thematic manipulation, of strict motivic economy, which he had acquired under Schoenberg's tutelage, with the principle of continuous transition. His music cultivates a favorite technique, probably dating back to the time of his studies: from each theme a remnant [*ein Rest*] is retained, ever smaller, until finally only a vanishingly small vestige remains; not only does the theme establish its own insubstantiality, but the formal interrelationships between successive sections are woven together with infinitesimal care. Berg's music, in all the lush opulence of its variety, cannot support naked contrast, the unmediated juxtaposition of opposites – as if the assertion of musical opposites might grant individual elements an existence incompatible with the metaphysical unpretentiousness, the fragile *ductus*, of all Bergian musical design. One can illustrate this Bergian manner – manner in the larger sense of Mannerism – with the children's game in which the word "Kapuziner" is disassembled and put back together again:

Alban Berg

Kapuziner – Apuziner – Puziner – Uziner – Ziner – Iner – Ner – Er – R; R – Er – Ner – Iner – Ziner – Uziner – Puziner – Apuziner – Kapuziner. That is how he composed, that is how all of his music plays in a Capuchin tomb of whimsy, and his development was essentially a development toward the spiritualization of that manner. Even in his late works – in which, not uninfluenced by twelve-tone technique, sharp thematic contours are occasionally sought, and in which the dramatist's penchant for characterization sometimes affects the absolute character of his music – even there the themes retain a suspended, indecisive quality, ever recalling the interval of a second through the use of minimal variation and rhythmic transformation. The wistful grace of the *Ländler* theme in the two clarinets, with which the Allegro of the Violin Concerto opens, seems to say that it, too, is not really a theme at all, that it has no intention of persevering, no wish to lay claim to itself.

Berg's affinity for Wagner is delineated by all of that, by the technique no less than the tone created by that technique. In contrast to others of his generation Berg took no part, either in aesthetic attitude or in technical procedure, in the opposition to Wagner. That provoked resistance. But Schoenberg's conviction that the idea of a piece of music counts for more than its style certainly applies to Berg. Since then the impotence of mere aesthetic ideology has become abundantly apparent. The question of quality has become far more urgent than that of means, means that are often enough adopted ready-made and which in and of themselves no longer attest either to courage or to strength. Music that is densely packed and organized down to the last sixteenth note has greater significance and proves more modern than music that flows along without hesitation because it is no longer even aware of the tensions inherent in its own material. Berg did not shrink from leading-tone effects or occasional triads, but he did disdain the kind of stylistic purity whose consistency comes at the price of clatter and impoverished language. His technique absorbed not only the Wagnerian legacy, but other elements, particularly the filigree texture common to the First Viennese School, as well as Debussy and much from German Expressionism. Most important, however, is that even in Berg the function of the Wagnerian component is altered through exaggerated, highly disturbing specialization. He did not illustrate the metaphysics of death; Schopenhauer played no role in the spiritual inventory of his maturity. Rather, the urge to vanish seizes music itself, which relinquishes claim to an independent world of ideas. Despite a completely different technical approach, Berg is in this respect related to his friend Webern, whose miniatures are just as intent upon falling silent as the large Bergian forms are upon self-negation.

Tone

Insofar as one still has an ear for such categories, what distinguishes Berg from Wagner is most apparent in precisely that Bergian tone (tone, incidentally, was Berg's favorite concept, one upon which he repeatedly based his musical judgments), a tone untouched by what from the outset characterizes Wagner's tone: self-glorification. Though traces of *Tristan* can always be detected in Berg, those of *Die Meistersinger* cannot. Not only does Berg's music never actually affirm themes; it absolutely never affirms itself. Any kind of insistence is foreign to it. With Berg, energy and activity were invested into the formative process; the results, however, have a passive, acquiescent, elusive quality. Berg's music never preens at its own reflection, but is, rather, characterized by the *gestus* of largesse, a *gestus* which was also peculiar to Berg's person and which rarely attained the kind of Wagnerian ecstasy that celebrates the moment of self-extinction as that of self-fulfillment. For Wagner the unconscious always represented the highest joy [*Höchste Lust*], whereas Berg's music renounces itself and the person speaking through it, in recognition of its inherent vanity, and perhaps also in the unacknowledged hope that only that which does not keep a grip on itself will not be lost. If one were to liken Berg to any previous composer, one would have to compare him with Schumann rather than Wagner. The way the end of the C major Fantasy opens into infinity, yet without transfiguring itself to the point of redemption, indeed, even without reference to itself: that anticipates the innermost essence of Berg's tone. By virtue of such affinity, however, Berg assumes a position in extreme antithesis to that which musical tradition calls healthy, to the will to live, to the affirmative, to the repeated glorification of that which *is*. This concept of health, inherently as ineradicable a part of prevailing musical criteria as it is of Philistinism, is in league with conformism; health is allied with what in life is stronger, with the victors. Berg abstained from such assent, as had the mature Schubert before him, as had Schumann, and perhaps also Mahler, whose music came down on the side of the deserter. While it may be true that, on the surface, his patiently and lovingly polished music has fewer sharp edges for the listener than has Schoenberg's, it is radical and shocking in its partiality for the weaker, the defeated: the figure of Berg's humanity. No music of our time was as humane as his; that distances it from humankind.

This identification with the defeated, with those who must carry society's burden, determined the selection of the texts for Berg's principal works, the two great operas. In the same spirit in which Karl Kraus invoked the bygone concept of humanity against the reigning inhumanity to which language had fallen victim, Berg seized upon Büchner's drama of the tortured paranoid soldier Wozzeck, who avenges the injustices done him

5

Alban Berg

by giving vent to his unrestrained nature and murdering his mistress; he seized upon Wedekind's circus tragedy of the irresistibly beautiful no-man's child Lulu, against whose unconscious omnipotence male society plots its revenge. Understandably, there is admiraton for *Wozzeck*'s scenic effectiveness, the product of the work's extremely taut construction, which, as it were, never allows the dramaturgic argument a moment's latitude. But such effectiveness would be unthinkable if Berg's constructive, musico-dramatic power were not joined with a spirit equating the human condition with suffering, a spirit that generally too easily falls victim to constructive considerations. This element in *Wozzeck* has acute contemporary relevance, for today music's right to exist hinges upon its success in giving definition to new characters [*Charaktere*]. A march penetrates into Marie's room, a musical diversion with an almost Mahlerian trio; but the strident march is askew, steeped in the mixed colors of a dream-like, alienated inwardness, as if perceived through the sightless panes of a tenement window. Thus the vulgar, blaring stage music is transformed into an archetype of the might wielded by military music over those whom it sweeps into a collective consciousness. Or, as in the symphonic centerpiece of the second act, there is a broadly drawn scherzo, tavern music with *Ländler* and waltzes, but of a profound, groping melancholy. The power of empathy is more all-embracing in *Wozzeck* than perhaps ever before experienced in opera: as if, in the place usurped in Wagner by the musical glorification of dramatic figures, there now remained nothing but compassion for them. Berg's intrinsic qualities can scarcely be better demonstrated than by comparing this tavern scene with Stravinsky, who comes to mind in the clouding and distortion of archaic forms of folk music. Yet in Berg there is no chillingly caustic wit, nothing malicious; the very fact that the merriment of such dances is false, that those caught up in it are cheated of it, that is what creates the deadly earnestness, creates, too, a multiplicity of layers transforming everything external into a metaphor for what is within, yet without forgetting how very much the mysterious, twisted inner world of those who are alienated from one another is itself simply the mark of their accursed outward existence. That is followed by a chorus of sleeping soldiers. Snores and groans are composed to show that for the unfree even sleep is warped; mutely a picture materializes of what enforced collectivization inflicts upon those incarcerated together in a barracks. And how effective, when, after the curtain rises silently upon the third act, Marie's weakly flickering, despairing yet consoling candle, and the wretchedly light, uneasy sleep of her child become music. *Wozzeck*: not the virtuoso application of the latest achievements to the long since dubious genre of grand opera, but rather the first paradigm of a music of genuine humanism.

6

Tone

In *Lulu* the self — from whose point of view events are seen, from whose perspective the music is heard — steps visibly onto the stage; Berg intimates as much with one of those quotations he loved to smuggle in, the way a medieval master included his self-portrait as a minor figure in a religious painting. Truly a corporeal-incorporeal suitor: united in Alwa's rondo themes is the exuberance of Schumannesque youth and Baudelairian fascination with fatal beauty. What became known as the first movement of the *Lulu Suite*, the enraptured praise of the loved one, glows in an ecstasy words cannot equal; as if the music wanted to become one of those fairy-tale gowns Wedekind envisaged for Lulu. This music, as a radiant, multi-hued jewel for the beloved body, seeks to restore human dignity to a banished, heretical yearning. Every bar of music intends salvation for the banished, for the symbol of sexual being, for a soul that in the hereafter rubs the sleep from its eyes, to quote from the most irresistible bars of the opera. In using and setting these words Berg paid his respects to the sixty-year-old Kraus, author of *Sittlichkeit und Kriminalität*. Berg's *Lulu* music thanks him in the name of that utopia which at heart motivates Kraus's critique of the bourgeois taboos that degrade love. Berg's music strikes a nerve where civilized man does not joke, and precisely this point becomes for him a refuge of the humane.

In this hymnic circus opera everything is sunnier, more supple, more elastic than in the earlier works: the *clair obscur* of Berg's orchestra is refined to a slender transparency reminiscent of Impressionism, only to surpass Impressionism's magic through greater sobriety and thus transport it into the spiritual. Seldom, to paraphrase Wagner, has the orchestra, has color, become so much part of the action as in *Lulu*; joyously the work abandons itself to the sensuous present it celebrates; once again scene and spirit are reconciled. The orchestration remained uncompleted. With Berg's death this most joyful creation succumbed to the worst of fates. Those who understand anything about theater must not deceive themselves into thinking that the fragmentary *Lulu* can only be resurrected intermittently, that it cannot be won for the repertoire, which needs this work if opera remains the least bit interested in demonstrating its right to exist as an institution. It is urgently to be hoped that the remaining portions of the third act will at last be orchestrated, if only to prevent the ambition and industry of belated defenders of the Grail from usurping a job for which they are not qualified.

To those given to categorizing, particularly in light of the euphoniousness of *Lulu* and the simplicity of the Violin Concerto, Berg could be seen as a moderate among the moderns, especially in the Schoenberg School, to which he remained absolutely loyal. He never completely severed ties with traditional means of tonality; his last piece, that very Violin Concerto, closes clearly in B♭ major with an added sixth. To be sure, Berg created some incredibly complicated structures very difficult to penetrate. But in general his art of transition [*Übergang*], mediation in a double sense, softens the shock. And thus, to his chagrin, audiences initially proved much more kindly disposed toward him than toward Schoenberg or Webern. That is why from the outset the specialists delighted in relegating him to the nineteenth century and in exempting their bright-eyed, bushy-tailed contemporaries from the Bergian melancholy, a melancholy which in the meantime has been only too fully justified by reality. Far from denying that element of temporal disjunction in his works, Berg himself highlighted it by orchestrating and publishing the romantic Seven Early Songs. But the tension between the familiar idiom and the unfamiliar, the unknown, was eminently fruitful: it was what called forth Berg's individual, recklessly thoughtful tone. Among the exponents of new music he was the one who least suppressed his aesthetic childhood, the *Golden Book of Music*. He ridiculed the cheap objectivity [*Sachlichkeit*] based on such suppression. He owes his concretion und humane breadth to tolerance for what has been, which he allows to shine through, not literally but recurrently in dream and involuntary memory. Until the very end he drew upon that inheritance and at the same time carried its burden, one that bowed his tall frame. It left its unmistakable physiognomic features on his work. Berg's impulse toward self-effacement, toward self-obliteration is, at its very core, one with the impulse toward extricating himself from mere life through a process of illumination and awakening; and the return of what has been, passive acceptance of the inescapable, contributes no less to that than did an ongoing spiritualization. Despairingly, his music accepted separation from the bourgeois rather than holding out false hopes of a state beyond the bourgeois, which to this day exists no more than does an alternative society. Alban Berg offered himself to the past as a sacrifice to the future. That is the source of the eternity within his present, the commencement of the endlessly mediated movement he invoked again and again.

Reminiscence

Trying to find words of remembrance for Berg is paralyzed by the fact that he himself had anticipated the exercise with macabre irony. When I was studying with him he occasionally amused himself during walks we took together around Schönbrunn by imagining the obituaries Viennese newspapers would one day have in store for him. He was convinced that one of them would confuse him with a Jewish folk humorist, by the name, I think, of Armin Berg; in another, a critic we knew all too well – one whose threat to write a book had to be forestalled by the 1937 volume published by Reich, Krenek, and me – would caw his *panegyricus* about the "Bard of *Wozzeck*": "As before him our Schubert, our Bruckner, our poor unforgettable Hugo Wolf, so now he, too, has died of hunger in his supremely beloved, unappreciative native city, which nonetheless carries him deep in her heart. Yet another link in the unending chain of immortals ..." The impossibility of banishing the nightmarish visions of this feverishly wakeful dreamer – visions that have meanwhile been far surpassed by the robust stupidity of the survivors who honor and label him – compels one to confront and examine them: not with reference to the world which they so accurately reflect, but with regard to the self concealed within them. Desperate humor was the satrap of death in a life that had grown around death as around its core. If anything, this desperate humor grew more intense. During the time of the Third Reich, when he buried himself in his house on the Wörthersee so as to be able to work undisturbed on *Lulu*, he called the place where he wanted to concentrate his "concentration camp." This remark was not cynical, it was morbid. Berg, who had no illusions as to what the National Socialists were all about, imagined how easily it could happen to him. Willi Reich tells how, while being taken to Rudolf Hospital during his last illness, he cracked jokes about its already being half way to the Central Cemetery; in the same context one should mention the story told about the unsophisticated Viennese blood donor when Berg's condition was already critical: "Let's just hope I don't turn into an operetta composer." This highly idiosyncratic quality is at the same

9

time eminently Austrian. Reading the narrative of Schubert's last days in Otto Erich Deutsch's superb documentation, one cannot escape the impression that precisely the bleak senselessness, the combination of sublime acquiescence and irresponsible indolence of that end was repeated in Berg's case, as if in his presence, that of the avant-gardist, the past had been suddenly resurrected. That is in no way out of keeping with his music. The identity of the city, her blessed, cursed incorrigibility, may have been of greater significance for the destiny of those two musicians than the hundred years separating them; one of the paradoxical conditons of Berg's modernity is that not so very much had changed.

He did not hesitate to apply irony to his own assessment of himself or a certain skepticism, which, in the form of patient self-criticism, became so extremely fruitful in his creative work. He once laughingly told me: "While composing I always feel like Beethoven, only afterwards do I realize that I am at best Bizet." In his distrust even of his own things one sensed a quality of self-alienation. It was with the expression of a sleepwalker laboriously awakening that Berg looked up and bestirred himself with gestures of a primeval majesty. After the Berlin premiere of *Wozzeck* and the dinner at Töpfer's where he was fêted and, like an embarrassed adolescent, scarcely able to respond, I was with him until late into the night, literally consoling him over his success. That a work conceived like Wozzeck's apparitions in the field, a work satisfying Berg's own standards, could please a first-night audience, was incomprehensible to him and struck him as an argument against the opera. That is how he always reacted. His affability never for a moment made compromises with the established order; quite without warning the recluse could explode all deceptive accord. At the Vienna performance of Mahler's Eighth Symphony under Anton Webern the two of us were almost thrown out for rowdiness. Berg was so carried away with enthusiasm for the music and its interpretation that he began to talk loudly about both, as if the performance were for us alone. It was not only in elevated moments that he showed this indifference toward what was happening around him. It was an immutable principle governing his life. Often I thought that nothing external, even things of consequence to him, could ever affect him to the core. Such inaccessibility proved to be a strength in his music. Equally at home with Strindberg and the orchestra of *Die glückliche Hand*, he was conscious even in the most intimate relationships of the ever present possibility of hatred and betrayal; that may not have been the least of his reasons for wanting to live permanently *in absentia*. On the other hand, he could enter cordially and gratefully into casual acquaintances; could praise provincial intellectual efforts, amazed that they were not altogether bad. He desired much, hoped for nothing, had therefore little to lose and even less to fear. His non-chalance was also imperturbability. If there is any truth to the facile associations between Wagner and Berg, then it would be a similarity with the Wotan of *Götterdämmerung*: not with the allegory of a self-negating world will − Berg negated that before he heard the first E♭ of *Das Rheingold* − but rather with the individualistic figure of the magnanimous, entangled, and weary god. Berg undercut the world's negativity with the hopelessness of his imagination, accepted it with the accumulated overflow and quintessence of Viennese pessimism, and with mockery and superstition as in those imaginary obituaries; that is how, in accordance with the Chinese proverb, the gentlest − shielded by his own defenselessness, the only armor granted the giant in modern times − could overcome the most obdurate. As a prisoner of his own physical being he had to die of an affliction in whose name the word "blood" resonates, a hermit's poison, born of his blood. Berg, whose tendency toward hypochondria was no less pronounced than the tendency to expect the worst from life, kept every possible illness in fanciful readiness for himself. The fact that he succumbed to one he misjudged and neglected, that he preferred not to see the danger or considered it exorcized by the date of the 23rd, the fateful number of his eccentric mysticism, that was the final melancholic subterfuge of an existence that for a half-century (as the subterfuge of a desperate man) had been able to maintain itself in music between sleep and death.

A national tradition, which he shared and at the same time kept at arm's length, that of "grumbling" [*Raunzen*], was coupled with his idiosyncratic defeatism, above all with the tendency to overrate his own imperfections and inadequacies, as if thereby to diminish them. To speak in psychological terms, one might well suspect that it was more a reaction to his own latent arrogance than some basic trait; pride and shyness were indissolubly linked in him. The line between seriousness and irony was constantly shifting, just as his irony was intertwined with modesty; whatever he said was as difficult to interpret as it is with well-bred Englishmen. His resemblance to Oscar Wilde was striking and he used it mischievously as an incognito; the word "Lord" cropped up frequently in his vocabulary. When I told him after my first meeting with Schoenberg that Schoenberg's appearance, in part because of the exaggerated elegance he cultivated at the outset of his second marriage, reminded me of a gypsy *primás*, Berg answered: "But he thinks he looks like a Lord." Berg's sense of humor was *humour noir*, his self-deprecation never entirely serious; there was not a trace of *rancune* or *ressentiment* in it. He rejected the anti-Semitism to which his Viennese surroundings could easily have tempted him, but not out of acquired insight; it was quite simply impossible for him. He considered himself entirely within the tradition of German music, but he included Mahler and Schoenberg as a matter of course. He was free from that raging *gestus* of "things must be different," which suggests itself so readily to all in Vienna who consider themselves neither Catholics nor Social Democrats. In order, incidentally, to understand correctly his concept, shared by Schoenberg, of the primacy of German music, it is necessary to remember that between the end of the First World War and the beginning of the Third Reich the international music scene, including the ISCM festivals, was dominated by a concessionary spirit of light, indeed superficial art, epitomized, for example, by the program of the Parisian *Les Six*, which was diametrically opposed to the radical modern movement. Paradoxically enough, at that time − the very period when the foundation was being laid in Germany for the gruesome dictatorship of political conformism − it was in fact German music that was non-conformist. Nevertheless, Berg the *artiste* recognized Baudelaire as his predecessor, no less than Proust did; the aria *Der Wein* is not only a prolegomenon to *Lulu*, but at the same time a declaration of affined solidarity. The French elements he introduced into German music, often mediated through literary impulses, surpassed the French themselves, including Debussy, whom he loved; even Debussy's [orchestrational] feasts and those of Ravel seem harmlessly bourgeois compared to the *Lulu* orchestra. In Berg, for the first time, there was a musical interpenetration of Austro-German and French elements of the sort that became common in music after 1945. Politically Berg was not really committed, but he felt himself to be a socialist insofar as in the twenties it behoved an orthodox reader of the *Fackel*. His emphatic Americaphilia was perhaps nurtured by the fact that one of his brothers lived there for many years. More than once I heard him say: if there *has* to be a technological civilization, then at least let it be radical and complete; his predilection, even aptitude, for what in America one calls gadgets, may have been a factor here. Unquestionably he gave some thought to the idea that in America he might extricate himself from the confining circumstances of even his best years and live more comfortably. With grim satisfaction he pointed to the success new music enjoyed there, for instance under Stokowksi, and used that as an argument against the Vienna Philharmonic. And yet his opposition to official Vienna had its Viennese provisos. When I, still very young and infected with the arrogance of opposition, refused for several months to attend the State Opera (which at that time I considered synonymous with the name Piccaver and his clique), he gave me a "dressing-down." So I went to the next performance that interested me, a *Salome* with Jeritza; I still remember it with horror, the term ham actor [*Kulissenreißer*] suited the then world-famous singer to a T. On the other hand, Berg often took me along to the Theater in der Josephstadt. I think he got tickets through the dramaturge Erhard Buschbeck, Trakl's friend, who had already demonstrated his courageous solidarity with Schoenberg and his friends at the first great Schoenberg scandal and with whom Berg maintained unbroken contact. Together we saw, among other things, the premiere of Werfel's *Juarez und Maximilian*. Berg's attitude toward Werfel was rather ticklish. Karl Kraus remained the unquestioned authority, but Werfel was Alma Mahler's husband and Berg liked his company, for in person he was thoroughly unpretentious and pleasant.

Berg's father was a Bavarian who had immigrated to Vienna from Nuremberg, but that did nothing to diminish Berg's *Wienertum*. He accepted what was Viennese as a God-given prerequisite. Accordingly he considered everything else provincial, even Prague, which seemed much more metropolitan in the twenties. Everything north German amused him no end. A mutual acquaintance, small in stature, was married to a very tall woman with a marked north German accent, and Berg took particular delight in making up imaginary love scenes between the two. We frequented a Berlin restaurant near the Opera because it was so near the rehearsals; but Berg not only considered it bad, he went on to generalize that Germans ate nothing but garbage; it would probably have been impossible ever to convince him otherwise.

I met him at the Frankfurt festival of the Allgemeiner Deutscher Musikverein in 1924, in the spring or early summer, on the evening of the premiere of the *Three Excerpts from Wozzeck*. Swept away by the work, I asked Scherchen, whom I knew, to introduce me to Berg. Within minutes it was arranged that I would go to Vienna to study with him; I had to wait until after my graduation in July. My move to Vienna was delayed until the beginning of January 1925. In Frankfurt my first impression of Berg had been one of extreme kindness, also of shyness, which helped me overcome the trepidation this object of my highest admiration would otherwise have instilled in me. If I try to recall the impulse that drew me spontaneously to him I am sure it was exceedingly naive, but it was related to something very essential about Berg: the *Wozzeck* pieces, above all the introduction to the March and then the March itself, struck me as a combination of Schoenberg and Mahler, and at the time that was my ideal of genuine new music.

Twice a week I made the trek out to Berg in Hietzing, Trauttmansdorff-gasse 27, the same first-floor apartment in which Helene Berg still lives today. At the time I thought the street incomparably beautiful. With its plane trees it reminded me, in a way I would find difficult to explain today, of Cézanne; now that I am older it has not lost its magic for me. When I went to Vienna again after my return from emigration and looked for Trauttmansdorffgasse I got lost and retraced my steps to my starting point at the Hietzing church; then I simply took off without thinking, blindly as it were, relying on my subconscious memory, and found my way there in just a few minutes. Before entering the house for the first time in 1925 I recognized where I was because of the dissonant chords (from the Chamber Concerto, to which at the time he was putting the finishing touches) that were being struck on the piano; I never dreamed that a very famous situation was repeating itself. The name on the door was designed by Berg in artistic script, just as on the original editions of Opp. 1 and 2, still with a trace of *Jugendstil*, yet clearly legible and without annoying ornamentation. Berg possessed an unmistakable gift for the visual arts. Actually, he was not primarily bound to musical material but motivated by the need to express himself. That he stayed with music was, considering his beginnings, almost accidental. To be sure, it cost him great effort to translate his general aesthetic expressive needs into something specifically musical: it was this trait he lent to Leverkühn. He was, above all else, an artist, but so much so that he became a highly specialized artist, a compositional master. At the same time he retained much of his sense for the visual, most noticeably in the calligraphic appearance of his full scores. He once spent an entire afternoon in the Café Imperial giving me a lesson in legible score writing. However, the visual aspect also extended into his composing as such. He laid out plans, which became ever more complicated, according to quasi-spatial symmetrical relationships. His propensity, too, for mirror and retrograde formations may, apart from the twelve-tone technique, be related to the visual dimension of his responses; musical retrograde patterns are anti-temporal, they organize music as if it were an intrinsic simultaneity. It is probably incorrect to attribute those technical procedures solely to the twelve-tone technique; they are derived not only from the microstructure of the rows, but also from the overall plan, as if from a basic outline, and as such they contain an element of indifference toward succession, something like a disposition toward musical saturation of space. There are models for that in the epic Mahler, as early as in the *Wunderhorn* songs. Much as Berg belonged to the tradition of thematic work and developing variation, that is, to a thoroughly dynamic kind of composition, his musical manner nevertheless had something peculiarly static about it, hesitantly marking time. Not until *Wozzeck* did his composing become more agile. It struck me that such stasis amidst kinetic activity revealed a kinship with Benjamin, who was enormously impressed with *Wozzeck*.

handicap his productivity. Striking, though, is his slow work pace; yet that was more the result of self-critical, thoroughly rational conscientiousness, however much this itself was related to anxiety neuroses. Berg sometimes reminded one of the boy who cried "wolf." In a letter he wrote me only a few weeks before his death he mentioned his furunculosis in passing and, preoccupied by my own affairs, I did not give this the attention it deserved. News of his death, which I received, after having already emigrated, while celebrating Christmas with my family in Frankfurt, was a blow for which I was unprepared. It is very possible that he paid too little heed to his last illness because he was accustomed to his own hypochondria.

All of that is a direct reflection of the *Jugendstil* element in his life, the *fin-de-siècle* that remained in his oeuvre to the very end and was so magnificently thematicized in *Lulu*. Physically he was like a paradigm of his music; he was still a scion of the generation of artists that wanted to emulate the wasted Tristan. Altenberg, of whom he saw a great deal in his youth, was for him one of Baudelaire's lighthouses. A word such as "secession" sounded contemporary when he said it; there were also connections with Schreker, just as there were between Schreker and Schoenberg. He had prepared the piano reduction of *Der ferne Klang*, a prototype of musical *Jugendstil*, and was a friend of a brother of the lovely Mrs. Schreker. One passage in *Wozzeck*, where the Captain sings that he, too, once experienced love, sounds like a Schreker parody; one usually parodies the things to which one is drawn, however ambivalently. That voluptuous, luxuriating note so inextricably a part of Berg's music and his orchestration also resonated in his longing for happiness. Paltry intellect, keen to ferret out weaknesses in even the most superior, sensed that side and wrought much mischief with it, finding fault in particular with the morbid aspects with which Berg's art dealt so creatively. The wholesomeness of now mature members of the youth movement [*Jugendbewegter*], as well as wise and omniscient music historians, constantly vent their spleen on Berg's neoromantic decadence, banishing him into the near past as a death-seeking individualist in order to sidestep what they do not understand about his so very complex body of works. The inexhaustible qualitative richness, the generous wealth of fully developed characters that serve Berg's idiom, are aimed at a level of subjective refinement that is wanting in most people today; its absence damns much of that subsequent proud "objectivity" as nothing but an empty shell, as an abstract negation of what one does not oneself possess. Berg's objectivity was of a different kind. Without doubt he was one of those modern artists who owes his stature to a sacrifice: namely, incorporating into one's self something foreign, something not quite assimilable. This was clearly apparent to false friends such as the

Alban Berg

treacherous Teuton Klenau and they believed thus to have discovered the Achilles heel of a man proscribed by the Hitler regime. Such arguments can be countered by pointing out that today's extremely dubious situation, as regards not only art but all intellectually significant creativity, forces art and creativity to repudiate themselves, to poison in order to preserve themselves, just as, from the point of view of reactionary banality, the late-Romantic Berg did when he threw in his lot with Schoenberg. It was strength, not weakness, when he shattered his already clearly defined artistic contour, when he forgot the aestheticizing youth depicted in early photographs: when he submitted to the teacher who was in many ways so repressive. Berg may not have fused the elements of his style seamlessly, but that in itself bears witness to truth: the renunciation of an aesthetically seamless unity in a world that tolerates continuity and totality only as a farce while crushing anyone attuned to the spirit. The fact that Berg, whose métier would have permitted him to eliminate all non-homogenous elements in his oeuvre, let them remain, with deliberate tolerance, almost montage-like, is more appropriate than if he had feigned an absolutely new beginning and thereby accepted an unexamined past. During my studies, in response to an impertinent question as to why there were tonal interpolations in most of his works, he answered without the slightest irritation or chagrin that this was simply his style and he did not choose to do anything about it. A traditional Austrian factor may have been at work here, the same aversion to force that motivated Hofmannsthal. Berg's commitment to the organic was so unswerving that he preferred to allow inorganic things to remain rather than rigorously or deliberately to re-form what had come to him through the reserves of his artistic experiences and, beyond that, of unconscious memory. It is unnecessary to gloss over inconcinnities, such as those in the Violin Concerto where the tonal harmonization of the Bach chorale is quoted; or the quasi-Straussian pattern from *Death and Transfiguration*, which in the second section employs dissonance as an allegory of the negative, consonance in the name of redemption, as if Berg's atonality had not long since invalidated that kind of polarity. But by realizing that what happens in the Violin Concerto happens despite and ultimately because of such inconsistencies [*Brüche*], by realizing how Berg's art of mediation, nowhere higher than in this last completed work, tested itself against what cannot be mediated, by realizing that, one can, on a higher plane, dismiss those ever intruding objections as pedantry. Berg is entitled to the kind of justice dispensed by Karl Kraus. Kraus mercilessly pursued every misplaced comma and yet was prepared to defend the most flagrant infraction of the rules when it resulted from a higher law of creation. Berg's stylistic inconsistencies [*Stilbrüche*] reflected an historical

20

tension within himself. The Violin Concerto, incidentally, was written very quickly; those who know Berg well will suspect that the often noted stylistic lucidity and clarification, which secured the work its popularity, had something to do with the pressures of composing on commission, out of which he made the virtue of a creative process at once less laborious and less inhibited. In that piece he wanted to make composing a little easier for himself, as in an orchestral interlude, and that led to many of the work's new perspectives; where Berg is said originally to have planned a sonata allegro as a symphonic centerpiece, he composed instead a long cadenza. In some of its simplest, intellectually most irritating passages, for instance the twofold quotation of the Carinthian folksong, the Violin Concerto acquires a heartbreaking emotive power unlike almost anything else Berg ever wrote. He was granted something accorded only the very greatest artists: access to that sphere, most comparable with Balzac, in which the lower realm, the not quite fully formed, suddenly becomes the highest. Berg had a deep affinity for Balzac, above all for *Seraphita*, a principal source for Schoenberg's theosophy and one that also left its trace on the *Jakobsleiter*. But the fact that Berg where he verges on kitsch also approaches the sublime is difficult to separate from his retrospective component: that is the factor that recalls the recent past. In aspects such as its sweeping, brilliant exaltation and dark precipitous plunge, situations of elevation and doom, all of *Lulu* is reminiscent of *Splendeurs et misères*, and those who lament this dimension instead of perceiving in it Berg's central significance will never understand this last opera. The way, however, in which the *imagerie* of the nineteenth century stirs within Berg is forward-looking. Nowhere in this music is it a matter of restoring a familiar idiom or of alluding to a childhood to which he seeks a return. Berg's memory embraced death. Only in the sense that the past is retrieved as something irretrievable, through its own death, does it become part of the present.

   Among the great composers Schumann was the one who – as in the slow pieces of *Kreisleriana* – discovered the musical *gestus* of remembering, looking and listening back. That, along with Schumann's impassioned exuberance, echoes throughout Berg's oeuvre, but in such a way as if the remembering power of music were as steeped in pain as is the prose of Proust – a prose which very much appealed to Berg and which bears a profound similarity to his carefully constructed, thicket-like, convoluted music. With Berg, the past survives in death's guise, attaining self-conscious awareness instead of being repressed. It not only salvages [*retten*] but illuminates the Büchner and Wedekind dramas he composed. In Berg's hands the nineteenth century is handled in such a way as to lend that century the very thing it is most persistently denied: style. Wedekind once said something to the effect that kitsch is the Gothic or Baroque of the modern period. This sentence, if regarded as something more than an *aperçu*, evokes something important about Berg's formal logic. That may well have been embodied in the Casti Piani scene of *Lulu*, of which the short variations of the Symphony give at least an indication; Berg considered that scene, which does seem to have been completely worked out in short score, "particularly successful." It would be utterly wrong to apply the term parody to such phenomena, as is the wont of writers on music. Berg loathed the term and once hauled me over the coals when I, unsure of myself, used it in presenting him with the setting of a children's poem. He liked the song: "It's good music, a lovely poem, and not in the least a parody." To heighten the illusion to the point of transparency: that was Berg's intention, that is how, without escaping, he freed himself from the spell of his parents. With unrelenting earnestness he surrendered to illusion as the form of truth most appropriate to himself.

This was only made possible through an intensification of compositional extremes that ultimately burst the bourgeois cultural boundaries within which Berg had grown up. In him the erotic urges of Tristan's world break through all individuation to the id. Psychology transcends itself in Berg's music. The staggering giant, awakening in the fissures of the 1880s, arose from strata of stone; no single force in his life was powerful enough to arouse him entirely from the deep sleep reflected in the first song of Op. 2. The threat that ugliness represented to Berg is expressed in his music, it generates fear and initially must have been perceived that way: the worst Schoenberg scandal was caused by one of the Altenberg Songs. The bridges to the past in Berg's music are slender, fragile planks: there are furious rapids below. Such was already the case in the intentionally amorphous Mombert song, which was reprinted by the radical *Blauer Reiter*; then in the second movement of the First Quartet; Berg let himself go with complete abandon in the March from the Three Pieces for Orchestra, an absolutely stupendous work, which has yet to be generally appreciated and whose analysis and explication must one day be the task of a definitive interpretation of Berg. When he showed me the score and explained it I remarked of the first visual impression: "That must sound like playing Schoenberg's Orchestral Pieces and Mahler's Ninth Symphony, all at the same time." I will never forget the look of pleasure this compliment — dubious for any other cultured ear — induced. With a ferocity burying all Johannine gentleness like an avalanche, he answered: "Right, then at last one could hear what an eight-note brass chord really sounds like," as if convinced no audience could survive such a sonority; that it did survive it and has in the meantime grown accustomed to much wilder things is surely a sign more of neutralization than of welcome progress in musical perception. If from a technical point of view Berg took his compositional departure from Schoenberg's First Quartet, the Chamber Symphony, and then *Pierrot*, his first loves nonetheless remained *Erwartung* and *Die glückliche Hand*; in his own music it was not inadequacies of form that dissatisfied him – that form, at which he labored with such infinite patience, as if out of fear – but rather the fact that his music no longer sounded as uncompromisingly naked as he probably wished. Nevertheless, a menacing quality can still be heard in the second act street scene of *Wozzeck*, in the Rondo of the Chamber Concerto, and in much of *Lulu*. That material, too, Berg did not so much "fashion," as *convenu* has it, as outwit. The very abundance of constructive forms, the incarnations of insatiability, tended toward the formless. My *prima vista* reaction to the March was somewhat unreflected but not completely false. Forming for Berg inevitably meant combining, also layering, synthesizing the incompatible, the disparate, and letting them grow together: de-forming. In his music the word "concrete" is given its true meaning. Once when I was working on a quartet movement with him and unable to reconcile variation and sonata form as I had intended, he immediately and, as it turned out correctly, advised that at the critical passage I bring two previous variations in counterpoint, that is, superimpose one upon the other. Berg was impervious to that commonplace of critical wisdom that music must be transparent – intoned ever since *Elektra*, but particularly during the twenties; the last words Max Scheler invented for himself, "more darkness," could as easily have been invented by Berg. With him all of Schoenberg's constructive techniques became a means for preserving anarchy. To be sure, they permeate the material, but with the exception of the Violin Concerto, they do nothing to help clarify it. Berg refused to let himself be tyrannized by popular contemporary slogans against complexity, he enjoyed a tangled snarl; he was only interested in transparency if he wished to present a rich texture so that it could be heard in all its detail; never as an end in itself. The organizational, rational principle does not eradicate chaos, if anything it heightens it by virtue of its own articulation. With that Berg realized one of Expressionism's most profound ideas; no other musician achieved that to the same degree.

For Berg was driven by the need to express himself, in all respects the opposite of Hindemith, with whom during his final years the isolated Berg seems to have had friendly contact. He professed to admire the way Hindemith's music flows on and on, in contrast to Berg's, which moves sluggishly; to be sure, it was never hard to convince him that such facility was of little value. The fact that Berg's need to express himself was stronger than a talent circumscribed by any one medium may have stemmed from his fundamentally undefined natural temperament. He measured and augmented his strengths against the difficulty of bonding himself to a medium. Initially he seems to have considered himself a poet and, like many highly gifted adolescents, including Wagner, only secondarily a composer. The magnificent artist did not take wing from the cocoon of craft. Nor did Berg play the piano with any virtuosity, indeed he distrusted (and rightly so) all composing based on instrumental facility. His literary sensibility is everywhere apparent, not least in his own prose. The article against Pfitzner with the ingenious analysis of "Träumerei," initially published in *Anbruch*, is without a doubt among the most significant essays on music, an argument for the fact that perception and experience are far more conducive to objectivity in musical judgment than run-of-the-mill aesthetic relativism would care to admit. Some theoretical passages by the dream-shrouded Berg offend those earnest bourgeois defenders of the irrationality of art because of what they chide as rationalism, though this rationalism is in fact a spiritual tenet holding that artworks are "manifestations of truth." In that spirit Berg possessed a lethal and incisive gift for – purely compositional – quotation, which was worthy of its model Kraus and musically quite original.

Berg's literary sensibility proved valuable to the composer in his choice of librettos for the two stage works and in their masterly operatic/dramaturgical adaptation. He felt that he was essentially an opera composer and disputed, though unjustly, having any lyrical instincts or fundamentally lyrical gifts. Around 1926 he planned to compose choruses to poems by Ronsard; Werfel and his wife had drawn his attention to them. Despite his excessive humility with regard to poetry, Berg was nonetheless expressing a well-founded perception: the supra-dimensional aspect of man and his musical responses resist traditional lyric brevity, and thus even in the *Wein* aria he combined three poems into an extended three-part form. The Clarinet Pieces are the exception that proves the rule. And yet he never thought monumentally in the *neudeutsch* sense. But his hesitantly expanding music required large surfaces; needed to take its time. He did not really tolerate an independent middle ground, no partial whole between atomistic detail on the one hand and a grand totality on the other; to him, the extremely small and the extremely large were complementary. Probably the underlying reason for his aversion to traditional lyricism was that he resisted finite, self-sufficient form altogether. His music is all transition. For all his absorption in detail, that quality he called jovial [*das Joviale*], a certain largesse, nonetheless infused his musical *gestus*; nothing was to be cut short, music was to hold nothing back. From the outset I considered that, too, similar to Benjamin and very different from Webern. Construction for Berg was always simply a matter of creating a maximum out of nothing and then retracting it; thoroughly paradoxical. Such self-destructive geniality, to set oneself impossible tasks and then *solve* them, required a capacity for obsessive tinkering. Berg's form types likewise gravitate toward opposite poles; toward stasis and imperceptible modification on the one hand, toward a breathless perpetuum mobile on the other. What lies between, the (Brahmsian) norm of graspable, clear-cut step-by-step progression, that was foreign to Berg, at least until *Lulu*. – In the private sphere, too, he liked to challenge life at its most refractory, as symbolized by technical gadgets such as an electric cigarette lighter, typewriter, or automobile, with which he was infatuated; technical clumsiness provoked his good-natured derision. He liked giving me advice on how to adjust my typewriter, nor was he above discussing the question of shaving. I, who considered the tedious procedure annoying, would have liked nothing better than a means to remove a beard once and for all, thus saving me the daily aggravation. In the true Altenbergian spirit Berg objected to such rationalism: what women liked about a smoothly shaven face was inseparable from the fact that they could feel the sprouting beard underneath. It was with such nuances that he discovered dialectics for himself. His patient attention to daily routine and his passionate attention to trivial activities became to no small degree a part of his music, the manic perfection of detail. It was precisely because his natural bent, the death instinct, drew him into diffuse, vast dimensions, that he was obsessed with craftsman-like integrity. A felicitous pedantry stands guard over his radical oeuvre as it did only once before over the works of the conservative Stifter. It was as if technical organization sought to restore in the work what life had withheld: Berg's music, in that regard quite defenseless, defends itself on all sides, refuses nothing, searches for the common denominator between expression and construction, combines the shock of chaos with the euphoria of ringing sound, autobiographical secrets with carefully planned architecture.

The criteria of his literary standards, exceptional among German musicians, surely came to some extent from Kraus; to no less an extent from his own disposition. In that regard at least he far surpassed Schoenberg and Webern; that was something Berg, the dramatist, could depend on, not only in the choice of the two subjects and in the theatrical instinct with which he adapted them, but even more in the relationship of his music to the texts. Benjamin, who was rather indifferent to music and who in his youth had nursed a certain animosity toward musicians, said to me with real insight after a performance of *Wozzeck* that as a composer Berg had treated Büchner's drama in a manner similar to Kraus's treatment of Claudius and Göcking. Berg's literary sensibility told him that one could not just compose these works the way Verdi did his librettos. The years separating a libretto and its musical setting are crucial for the composer, who must establish a certain distance to it through the principle of stylization. It is difficult to say whether such distance is the prerequisite for the objectifying process in Berg's operatic compositions, or whether that process itself created the distance. In any case, perhaps with dawning presentiment of the problematic nature of opera today, he sensed that this genre would not necessarily remain productive, though he energetically disclaimed entertaining any ideas of operatic reform. The quality of the texts he chose may have induced him to pay them the homage of not simply subordinating them to music as if they were defenseless. His treatment of them was governed by the partiality common to men of literature for "salvaging" [*Rettung*], a literary tradition dating back to antiquity. Admirable the care with which Berg adapted both texts without violating them, the way he prepared them for composition, without, however, exempting so-called lyricism from a no less conventionally conditioned "interpretation" [*Reflexion*]. He was undecided whether to compose Hauptmann's *Pippa* or *Lulu*. In a postcard of 11 January 1926 Soma Morgenstern advised him to composer *Pippa*, and Berg asked for my opinion. In November 1927 I received a letter from him, the most important passage of which read: "... I have decided to begin composing an opera this coming spring. I have 2 plans in mind, of which I will *certainly* execute *one*. So it is simply a question of *which one*. For this purpose I am also asking you for advice: Namely: either *Und Pippa tanzt* or *Lulu* (the latter as a result of combining *Erdgeist* and *Büchse der Pandora* to make a 3-act (6–7 scenes) libretto). What do you think? Since I will definitely compose one (or possibly both), it only remains to decide *which one* of the two (or possibly which one *first*) ..." At the top of the page containing the *Lulu* plan Berg requested strictest confidence. I cannot say with certainty whether it was I who first pointed him toward *Lulu*, as it now seems to me upon reflection; in such cases it is easy to err out of narcissism. In any case I brought all my arguments to bear on behalf of the Wedekind opera, and doubtless convinced the man of the theater by pointing out dramaturgical weaknesses in the glassworks fable, which loses its focus after an inspired first act that veritably cries out for music. It was my impression that Gerhart Hauptmann, to whom Frau Mahler introduced Berg in Santa Margherita, did not particularly appeal to him. Hauptmann had long since fallen into disfavor with Kraus, who, on the other hand, retained a lifelong esteem for Wedekind. Berg's attitude toward Kraus was one of unqualified veneration; whenever I was in Vienna we attended together every Kraus lecture we could. However, I do not believe that Berg, who knew Kraus well but was loath to enter the sphere of importunate admiration, ever met with him in those years. On the other hand, he liked to send Kraus splendid atrocities, occasionally "expanded and elaborated," from music journalism; no doubt more than one such quotation found its way into the *Fackel*. During Kraus's lectures Berg occasionally flirted with his own slowness, declaring he could not quite grasp extremely pointed poems after just one hearing. His relationship to Kraus was as toward an authority; for Berg, as for the circle around George, the word master was still absolutely appropriate for an artist. I once spoke of Hofmannsthal and his *Der Turm*, and of the possibility of composing the *Neue Deutsche Beiträge* version of the tragedy. Even today I believe no subject was more eminently suited to him than this one or the related material of Kaspar Hauser. But as a loyal *Fackel* reader he wanted nothing to do with Hofmannsthal, and would not for the world have admitted that there was any other side to Hofmannsthal than that of the Salzburg Festival. There was but a single, quasi-Proustian connection between the two: a maid served successively in both households.

His relationship to contemporary composers was similarly selective; he acknowledged very few. He longed for musical standards similar to the literary ones established by Kraus; as a matter of fact, Schoenberg's impact on his circle had very much that effect. What he did not like about Krenek, who was his friend, was a certain unwieldiness and, if one may say so, technological irrationality: where one expects a sequence, he once said, there's none, and where one does not expect it there is. No doubt he changed his opinion when Krenek adopted the twelve-tone technique. He loved Webern without reservation, yet with an underlying note of mockery, as if in subtle revolt against orthodoxy; fanaticism was foreign to him. He made fun of Webern's brevity, especially when it turned out that his twelve-tone pieces were scarcely longer than the earlier ones, whereas according to Erwin Stein's Schoenberg-inspired manifesto one of the very tasks of the new technique was to enable composers to write more extended forms again. Together we once concocted a Webern parody, consisting of a single quarter-note rest under a quintuplet bracket and garnished with every conceivable symbol and performance notation, which, to top it off, was then to fade away. Berg despised mediocre composers without a second thought; he could amuse himself by weighing which of two moderately modern Viennese was worse, the one belonging peripherally to the Schoenberg School, the other to another school — he finally decided in

Alban Berg

favor of the one from his own; today he would probably think differently. He defended Reger, whose works were given a significant role in the programs of the Society for Private Musical Performances, but he conceded without much protest that in the mature works any bar of one piece could be transposed to any other. What he thought of Pfitzner is documented in the well-known polemical article; this article epitomized the ideal of a musical *Die Fackel*, which inspired the periodical *23* edited by Willi Reich; it was probably Berg's idea. He once spent a couple of days with Pfitzner at the home of Frau Mahler and was grimly amused to observe Pfitzner hiding his works-in-progress to keep Berg from stealing anything. Berg's relationship to Mahler was enthusiastic and without reservation, above all with regard to the later works. We often played the four-hand arrangement of the second *Nachtmusik* from the Seventh, as well as much else by Mahler. In fact, he cultivated this by now probably extinct art; he had practiced it since childhood with his sister Smaragda. She resembled [Stefan] George the way Berg resembled Wilde. Wagner was inviolate. Occasionally Berg had me orchestrate passages from *Götterdämmerung* in order to compare the results with Wagner's, an extraordinarily instructive undertaking.

He thought a great deal of Bartók and was unabashedly proud when he recognized the influence of the *Lyric Suite* on Bartók's Fourth Quartet. He was a little hurt that Bartók, who occasionally came to Vienna, never troubled to look him up or anyone else from the Schoenberg circle. But the two had incompatible temperaments, Berg's urbanity and the Hungarian's cool correctness verging on the inflexible. Stravinsky did not occupy a prominent place in Berg's intellectual inventory, though he *did* think highly of the *Three Japanese Lyrics*, which border on Schoenberg. He had a soft spot for Suk — was, in fact, very much drawn to the Czechs. The great composers of the standard repertoire were sacrosanct to him, as they were to the entire Schoenberg School; unquestionably he would have rejected the notion that new music, regarded objectively, is at the same time a critique of traditional music. He was passionate in his loyalty to Schumann; his favorite song was the little-known "So oft sie kam." He was not unaware of the relationship between his own tone and Schumann's. What today passes for "Baroque music" left him cold; for him, music began with Bach. He took no exception to disparaging remarks I made about Bruckner, though surely he saw through the immaturity of my opinions. He left correction to development: which did not happen until after his death, under the unforgettable impression of Webern's performance of the Seventh in London.

Even during his lifetime people liked to play off the more accessible Berg against Schoenberg. That was particularly repugnant to him. Berg's

28

position with regard to Schoenberg can probably be summarized by saying that Schoenberg envied Berg his successes, while Berg envied Schoenberg his failures. He was aware of a certain jealousy on Schoenberg's part. And he himself criticized a want of expressive content in Schoenberg's first twelve-tone compositions; later on Schoenberg recaptured that expressivity, only to have the flaw re-emerge all the more ominously across the full range of his creative activity after 1945; at times the Kranichstein generation lashed out against the *style flamboyant*. However, Berg retained his tolerant attitude, even in the face of stylistic changes in his teacher that may have dismayed him; he argued that the initial price for every new technique must be a certain decline in content, which is sure to develop eventually. He did not live to experience the phase in Schoenberg where precisely that occurred. On the other hand, he was seriously irritated by Schoenberg's idiom, his "tone" – that element of insistence, advocacy, righteousness; for instance in the introductory bars of the March in the "Serenade." It was ever Berg's way to put himself in the wrong and, by being *a priori* convinced of the world's superior strength, thus give it the slip.

When I first came to Vienna I imagined the Schoenberg circle to be fairly tight-knit, similar to the George circle. Even then that was no longer the case. Schoenberg, remarried, lived in Mödling; his elegant young wife, so it seemed to the old guard, kept him rather isolated from the friends of the old heroic days. Webern probably already lived out in Maria Enzersdorf. They did not see much of one another. Berg particularly lamented the fact that he so seldom saw Webern and Steuermann, of whom he was very fond, and blamed it on Vienna's size, which was hardly formidable. But deep down it may have been his tolerance [*Liberalität*] that subtly separated him from the other Schoenberg students, and probably also the need of this extremely sensitive and vulnerable man to avoid as far as possible the tyranny of the collective. I met Schoenberg through Berg one Sunday in Mödling where Webern was conducting Bruckner's F minor Mass in a church. Closer acquaintance first came about in the Wiedner Hauptstrasse apartment of Kolisch's mother. Berg took me along one evening. On that occasion the Kolisch Quartet played Beethoven's F minor Quartet, Op. 95, in a truly innovative interpretation coached by Schoenberg.

At that time Berg and his wife frequently socialized with Ploderer, a lawyer devoted to the Schoenberg circle. He was friends with Soma Morgenstern, whose Polish musicians' circle included, among others, Jascha Horenstein and Karol Rathaus. Morgenstern's brilliance and wit deeply impressed Berg, which is why – though I liked him very much – I was probably jealous of the older and more worldly man. At times Berg no doubt relegated my own philosophical ballast to the category he termed

29

"a bore" [*fad*]; I joked about it once and he did not seriously contradict me. "A bore" as a collective term for anything not sensuously appetizing was in fact one of Berg's favorite words. Admittedly I was deadly earnest in those days, which could get on a mature artist's nerves. Out of pure veneration I tried never to say anything I did not consider particularly profound, though I did not always live up to that standard; I had as yet no idea that in their contact with others, emphatically productive people prefer to relax from those extremes of intensity and concentration which at the time I considered their due.

Berg introduced me into the home of Alma Mahler so that I could play through the part of Marie for the singer Barbara Kemp, who was originally to create the role in Berlin in December 1925; in the end she did not do so. When Berg and I met Kemp some time later she walked up and down Unter den Linden with us, tirelessly repeating how she was working on a completely new interpretation of Carmen, interpreting her as a whore. Obviously Frau Mahler did not correspond to the *imago* a twenty-one-year-old associated with the name. That first afternoon she said to me: "Last night I told Beer-Hofmann: 'Kids, one thing you ain't got, and that's blood [*Kinder, euch fehlt oans, 's Blut*].'" Berg laughingly listened to what I had on my mind, indirectly agreeing. Nonetheless I thought I owed it to him to say a few admiring words about her oft-praised vitality, although I certainly did not consider Frau Mahler any longer attractive. Berg picked up on that and asked me to write, for she had departed for Venice, and tell her what I had told him. I did so and received an extremely cordial reply by return post; as a matter of fact, two weeks later I received a second, almost identical letter, nearly verbatim, if anything even more cordial: obviously she had forgotten having already written me.

In any case, it is thanks to Frau Mahler that Berg, at a time when he was in financial straits, was able to publish the piano score of *Wozzeck*. Berg's parents were apparently well-off, though not wealthy; otherwise the family's circumstances would not have become precarious immediately after the father's death. The situation remained that way, with ups and downs, except for a few years between the premiere of *Wozzeck* and the outbreak of German fascism. Berg's external life was eked out in the face of adversity and overshadowed by it; among all the good things Helene Berg did for him, surely not the least was that it was essentially she who managed the problems in such a way as to make them imperceptible. No one but that proud woman could tell of the privations those two secretly suffered, how much time they lost over worries which are a disgrace for the world in which they lived. But for the individual, poverty and wealth do not necessarily correlate directly to actual assets, certainly not among the bourgeoisie.

Reminiscence

I have known people, a famous university professor, a high-ranking radio administrator, who earned a great deal of money and were still unable to shake off an air of poverty and neediness. On the other hand, there are those who have barely enough and yet never give the impression of poverty. Berg was one of those. The atmosphere always had something upper-class about it, to use the term in its proper sense. This was primarily because of the matter-of-fact attitude of those accustomed to a good life; just as formerly wealthy immigrants had an easier time dealing with unaccustomed neediness and complained less than did the petty bourgeoisie. Moreover, there was a certain hard-to-define *gentlemanly* and *ladylike* quality about the two, beginning with their very appearance. The less conscious of it they were, the greater the effect. Nothing in their lifestyle was Bohemian. Rarely have I seen a home in which I felt more comfortable; there was something spacious, large, corresponding precisely to Berg's ideal of the jovial. Their existence was made easier by the fact that long after the First World War ended, Austria, still not thoroughly capitalized, afforded intellectuals cozy little nooks in which to winter with some degree of comfort; the Social-Democratic city administration, for instance, helped with rigorously enforced rent control. Privately I did wonder, as incidentally I wondered about many Viennese with free-lance careers, what Berg lived on before the time of his great success. He taught only a few students, his fees were modest compared to what was then customary in Germany. Something still remained of the family fortune, particularly the Carinthian property. Between 1928 and 1933, approximately, perhaps a bit earlier, Universal Edition paid him a fixed advance. Like Schoenberg, he was attached to that firm, particularly to its director Hertzka, who did indeed demonstrate an extraordinary instinct for the great compositional talents of his own generation and the next one. Berg suffered after he was condemned by the National Socialists as a cultural Bolshevist and his works no longer brought in royalties. His lifestyle had expanded after *Wozzeck*; he took pleasure in a little car which, as far as I know, he kept until the end. After 1933 the sale of Berg's manuscripts became one source of income; I myself tried in vain to interest an English Maecenas in that of the *Lyric Suite*; that project was a major topic in the last letters he wrote me. Louis Krasner's commission, which led to the composition of the Violin Concerto, though also to the interruption of the *Lulu* orchestration, came as a great relief. That year for the first time he spent the entire winter in Berghof [Waldhaus] probably because it cost scarcely anything to live there. It is a depressing aspect of Berg's biography that it was probably in order to save money that he did not immediately call on the best available doctors to treat his furunculosis, although an attitude of "nothing can be done about it"

Alban Berg

[*Da kann man halt nix machen*], of resignation, perhaps his own weariness, also contributed to his death. In the face of the millions of murders committed by National Socialism one forgets the more subtle misdeeds of the Third Reich: had it not established itself Berg probably need not have died. Even in his death panic joined with gentleness, hideous consistency with the unfathomable.

To describe the teacher is difficult for me because what he taught me became so integral a part of my musical being that even today, forty years later, I have yet to gain any critical distance. When I came to him I had learned in private study with Bernhard Sekles the kinds of things one learns in a conservatory, with the exception of four-part Palestrina counterpoint, which I made up later. After the first lesson, during which I showed him a few things, Berg decided against formal instruction, not even the study of form or what at the academies is considered "free composition," but rather just to discuss my own things with me. In order to get an idea of what it was like to study with him one must have a sense of his particular brand of musicality. Even as a teacher he responded slowly, almost broodingly, his strength was that of intellectual imagination and an acutely deliberate command of the possibilities, as well as a strong original fantasy in all compositional dimensions; not one among the newer composers, not even Schoenberg or Webern, was so much the antithesis of the ideologically puffed-up musician of that period as he was. Usually he would take a long time looking at what I brought him and then come up with possible solutions, particularly for passages where I had reached an impasse. He never smoothed over difficulties or skirted them with facile answers, but always hit the nail on the head: he knew better than anyone that every properly composed measure represents a problem, a choice between evils. Systematically he cultivated in me a feeling for musical form, inoculated me against what is insufficiently articulated, against idle activity, above all against mechanical, monotonous rudiments in the midst of compositional materials cut loose from their moorings. Whatever he demonstrated in specific cases was of such self-evident clarity that it made an indelible impression. For instance, in the accompaniment to a song of which I was very fond, he objected to the excessive use of major thirds, a general tendency of mine at that time, and in so doing cured me once and for all of harmonic padding. He strongly urged a multiplicity of differing ideas, even in the most compressed space, though in such cases ever ready to mediate between them. Each of his corrections bore an unmistakably Bergian character. He was much too well-defined a composer to be able, as the saying goes, to put himself in another's place; in the pieces he

32

worked on with me any fairly knowledgeable person could easily identify the passages for which he was responsible. But much as these solutions were his own, they nevertheless attest to an equally strong compulsion toward objectivity and were never simply grafted on. With loving care he devoted himself to freeing me of my compositional inhibitions, just as — very different from the way Schoenberg treated his students — he always encouraged me; in fact, I think he disapproved of my doing anything but composing. In order to prevent my getting too involved in details at the expense of overall coherence, or in order to keep a piece going when I was ready to despair, he advised me to write out just one or two voices over long stretches, possibly even without specific notes, just rhythms or contour, neumatic sketching, as it were; later I transferred that trick to my literary technique. What he transmitted to me by way of instruction had the unmistakable character of doctrine, of the authority of "our school." In the name of that school he saw to it that as of the first lesson, quasi symbolically, I placed an accidental before every note: sharp, flat, or natural. The main principle he conveyed was that of variation; everything was supposed to develop out of something else and yet be intrinsically different. Unlike Schoenberg he had little use for stark juxtapositions. He taught me no small number of more or less fixed rules, which of course required modification and were not meant to be inflexible, but which, by their very drastic character, were pedagogically quite useful and supplied a means of justifying whatever one was striving for. Thus he firmly distinguished between two kinds of composition: symphonic, dynamic, richly organized music and that which, possibly using one of Schoenberg's terms, he called the "character piece," in which, ideally, a single strongly defined trait serves to set it apart from what follows; the models Berg cited for this were Schoenberg's George Songs and *Pierrot*.

In later years, with growing knowledge of the world and as if in compensation for his increasing isolation, Berg developed a kind of diplomatic life strategy, not dissimilar to, though more successful than, the way Benjamin would have liked to live. I called him the foreign minister of the land of his dreams and he laughed. There were not many *Wozzeck* performances where he did not give his photograph with a generous inscription to the principals, especially the conductors. More than one conductor today can boast of Berg's having declared that *his* performance was the best there ever was; actually, he probably considered the only authoritative performance to have been the one under Erich Kleiber. But this attitude of the mature Berg was not cynical. Probably without even being aware of it, he gradually learned to put his generous, cordial friendliness, which was fundamentally at odds with reality, at the service of that reality; I have often observed the same in other shy, vulnerable people. So implacable was his antagonism to the established order, so strongly did he consider his successes to be based *a priori* on a misunderstanding, that he developed stratagems as his basic human right. Those who want to moralize about that become spokesmen for a world that undermines candor the more it demands it. Berg turned the world's own weapons against it. In taking up his monadological position he followed the world's game rules of inviolable self-preservation of the individual, and thereby defended his integrity. In the eleven years I knew him I always sensed more or less clearly that as an empirical person he was not entirely present, not entirely involved; it occasionally became apparent in moments of abstraction, which corresponded with the absent expression of his eyes. He was not at one with himself in the way the existentialists extol as ideal, but had instead a peculiarly impregnable quality, indeed something uninvolved, observer-like, of the kind that Kierkegaard, merely out of Puritanism, decried in aestheticism. Even passion, at the moment he abandoned himself to it, became material for his art; Wagner probably did not behave very differently when he fled both wife and mistress in order to write the last act of *Tristan* in Venice; Thomas Mann, Gide, and Proust have made similar observations. Berg's empirical existence was subordinate to the primacy of creative work; he honed himself as its instrument, his store of life experiences became solely a means of supplying conditions that would permit him to wrest his oeuvre from his own physical weaknesses and psychological resistance. He was at all times so aware of the imminence of death that he accepted life as provisional, entirely focused on what might remain, though without severity or egoism. In Berlin he once risked his own life to snatch someone from the rails of the subway who would have been crushed only seconds later. In essence he was prepared to give away everything he had, even that most precious thing, his time. His aloofness from humanity was more humane than that which among humans is considered humane. Narcissistic and selfless at the same time, he did not clutch at his life, which seemed subject to a proviso clause. That probably explains his irony. If it be true that intellectuals should not be fathers, then Berg was the most unfatherly man one could imagine; his authority was the total absence of authoritarianism. He successfully avoided becoming an adult without remaining infantile.

The works

Analysis and Berg

Berg was well disposed toward analysis. His characteristically painstaking analyses of Schoenberg's works, of *Gurrelieder, Pelleas und Melisande,* and the First Chamber Symphony, were completed as a young man. Though published, they are not nearly as well known as they deserve to be; in particular the analysis of the Chamber Symphony, a work that remains difficult even today, can be considered exemplary; a collected edition would be well worthwhile. His essay on Schoenberg's D minor Quartet opened perspectives for an entire book on that work, one that unfortunately remained unwritten; in addition to all its other merits, the analysis of "Träumerei" applies very profitably the experience of the Schoenberg School's motivic-variational thinking to a work of traditional music. It is one of the few texts which answers conclusively or, to use one of Berg's favorite words, "unconditionally" [*verbindlich*], the question as to why a particular work of art can with reason be called beautiful. The Schoenberg School's concept of the objective quality and objective criteria of something composed is in accordance with the fact that, strengthened by their own self-critical exertion, they do not surrender musical judgment to the kind of emotion that is often nothing more than a dull mixture of reactions inappropriate to the object itself. In a compositional process in reverse, as it were, beginning with the end product, it is necessary to determine the objective properties of a composition's quality by immersing oneself in the work as a whole and its microstructure. In truth, any interpreter who is musical and seriously committed to the subject at hand learns for himself that there is no other way faithfully to describe texture, economy, stratification, and coherence than through the kind of analysis described above. Distrust of analysis – usually beginning, as the example of Freud has shown, with a distrust of the word itself – is not only allied with an uncritical, irrational view of art but also with a reactionary attitude in general. That attitude imagines cognition to pose a threat to substance, whereas in fact what is lasting is demonstrated only by its capacity to disclose itself through penetrating cognition. Whether in reality or in their imagination foes of analysis confuse the rationality of the cognitive process — which is self-evident to the point of pleonasm — with a rationalistic view of the object of cognition; the method is erroneously and directly equated with the very object it is attempting to approach. The surest symptom of such bourgeois irrationality, which sets art apart as an ideological complement to prevailing economic and social pseudo-rationality, is the idiotic and ineradicable argument to which the analyst is automatically subjected: whether the composer was aware of the connections revealed by the analyst, whether they were intended. In art everything depends on the final product, the artist being its organ; it is nearly impossible to reconstruct convincingly what he himself had in mind, but it is also largely irrelevant. The work itself, by virtue of its own inherent logic, imposes certain features upon its author, its executor, without his even having to reflect upon it. The more completely the artist distances himself from the matter, the better the work. The artist's acquiescence to the demands presented to him, beginning with the first bar, carries incomparably more weight than his intentions. Schoenberg provided wonderful examples for this, especially in the First Chamber Symphony.

To be sure, the concept of analysis must maintain sufficiently high standards if it is not to degenerate into bad rationalism. Analysis focuses on those concrete moments that make up a piece of music. Its measure is not the reduction of those moments to more or less abstract rules, which within given idioms are fairly identical; otherwise, to quote Metzger, analysis becomes tautological. It must be concerned with the flesh, not the skeleton. Though it is impossible, especially in traditional music, to disregard certain abstract, more or less invariant structural characteristics, whose meaning is in lively interaction with the fibre, no one has ever understood a work by simply reducing it to such abstract primary entities. Rather, it is more important to determine the changing values of those abstract characteristics within the constellation of each individual work; accordingly, as a result of such changes even abstract invariants take on radically different meanings. Berg did not, as the literal mind might think, simply avail himself of the rondo form in the last scene of Act II in *Wozzeck*, or in the finale of the Chamber Concerto: by virtue of the function this traditional form assumes in these pieces it becomes something quite different in each case, something distinct from the traditional type. Important as was Heinrich Schenker's contribution in shaping musical analysis into an instrument for the perception of musical processes, or, as he so rightly calls it, of the musical "content" — as opposed to the literature of thematic guides and poeticizing description — the similarity among his so-called *Urlinien*, his eager protestations notwithstanding, is an argument against their fecundity. His analyses end in universality, not in the specifics of an individual work. To say that the greatness of great art resides in such universality is a desperate apologia. Schenker considers the essence of a work of art to be those qualities that are general and unvarying, in keeping with his, musically speaking, reactionary attitude: with his idolization of tonality. His method (developed, not incidentally, from Beethoven's music – where tonality itself was, as it were, "thematic," not just the prerequisite for the composition, but also confirmed by it) cannot be applied to the best products of new music such as the works of Berg, in which traditional categories and the tonal idiom, deep as their traces may be, are broken from the outset by an emphatic tendency toward particularization.

The *raison d'être* of analysis, which vulgar prejudice prefers to reject as an atomistic undertaking, as dismemberment of form, lies in that quality of "having-been-constructed" which no organized music can cast off, and which is, in fact, true of the canonized works of tradition to an incomparably greater degree than the prevailing art cult finds convenient. Analysis retaliates against musical works of art by pointing out that they are truly "composed," assembled from components; the illusion they generate – that of an absolutely integrated being, of the necessary sequence of the whole and its flow – offsets their own constituent parts. Analysis, being the destruction of that illusion, is critical. Enemies of analysis are well aware of that. They want nothing to do with it, fearing that in forfeiting the illusion of the absolute meaningfulness of the whole they will be robbed of some secret within the artwork which they think they hold and must protect, but which is largely synonymous with that illusion. At the same time limits are thus set for the usual kind of analyses, including those I contributed to Reich's 1937 Berg book, which now reappear here. To be sure, this does not mean, as prejudice would have it, that *less* analysis is needed, but rather *more*, a second reflection. It is not enough to establish analytically the constituent elements, nor even the most concrete primary cells, the so-called "inspired ideas." Above all it is necessary to reconstruct what happens to those ideas, or, to use Schoenberg's phrase, to write the "history of a theme." With Berg, in particular, traditional analysis of elements misses the mark because – and this is an extremely characteristic feature – structurally his music does not consist of elements in any commensurably traditional sense. It is, by its inherent nature, in a constant process of disintegration. It strives toward the individual element as its goal, that is, toward a threshold value bordering on nothingness. That is the technical corollary of what has been interpreted as the death urge in Berg's music. In many respects his idiom is closer to tonal music than is Schoenberg's

Alban Berg

or Webern's, but in *this* dimension his rejection of it is more categorical than that of his friends. While he adopted the technique of "developing variation" from Schoenberg, he unconsciously steered it in the opposite direction. Generating, according to Schoenberg's idea, a maximum of shapes from a minimum of elements is just one level of Berg's compositional technique; the other lies deeper: that music, by its very process, dissolves. It ends in the minimum, virtually in a single note. In that way the components grow to resemble one another in retrograde, satisfying the principle of economy in reverse. With Berg, probably more than with any other composer, the kind of element that analysis reveals is not a first step, a point of origin, but rather the result, entirely a product of internal mediation. The agenda for future, satisfactory understanding of Berg would be the analysis of that mediation [*Vermittlung*], possibly related to what I have attempted to show in the destiny of certain thematic shapes in Mahler and in the interpretational analysis of Berg's Violin Concerto in *Der getreue Korrepetitor*. At some point the concept of analysis as applied to Berg will have to be turned around in the same way his music turned from the whole to the smallest entity (in which the whole disappears) as its end. It is well known and well documented that Berg loved to pick up musical categories from the past and subject them to extreme metamorphosis. One such category of Viennese classicism would be what has come to be known, possibly in a term coined by Schoenberg, as a field of static suspension [*Auflösungsfeld*]: those characteristic bars toward the end of a sonata exposition, before the coda, in which motivic activity, often on the dominant, gives way to purely harmonic activity, with trills over the dominant. Berg extended the use of such fields of static suspension as a formal device throughout a composition, fused with the motivic technique of "remnants" [*Reste*] and with the principle of musical differentiation; essentially the entire movement becomes its own field of static suspension.[1] He elevates what was at one time incidental and conventional to fundamental significance and, through consistent use, transforms it into the means by which – with inexorable tenderness – convention is destroyed.

---

1 French Impressionism occasionally ventured just as far in its tendency toward static suspension, for instance in the second volume of Debussy's piano Preludes; the affinity is readily apparent and has not escaped the commentators. The difference is therefore all the more critical. Debussy, whose compositional approach was profoundly static, presented a field of static suspension and its elements as something completed, already established. Berg is a link in the German tradition of "developing variation" to the extent that he not only produces that result, the fields of static suspension, down to their differentials, but structures and presents the process of their becoming, their dissolving, as the essential content of the composition.

Analysis and Berg

Analysis of Berg's music finds itself in the peculiar situation that, to a certain extent, the music effects its own analysis. On the one hand Berg's technical inclinations suggest that his music, as an unrelenting and permanent process of becoming, continually fragments itself into the smallest entities. On the other hand, because of its infinitesimal nature, this smallest entity can really no longer be regarded as an element, as is usually the case in analyses. That implies nothing less than that, in terms of the structural aspect of *becoming per se* (a becoming that resists all consolidation and thereby revokes its own structure), Berg's music, in relation to all other new music, offers something radically new. This is apparent only after reflection upon its suitability for analysis. The idiosyncracy of Berg's music is that, owing to its act of permanent self-production, owing to the fact that the creative process becomes, as it were, identical to the creation itself, the music transcends to nothingness. It describes a double movement. Its basically analytic technique threatens it with the undifferentiated sameness of that into which it dissolves; but in order to achieve articulation of precisely this process there is a need for heightened constructive plasticity. The indistinct becomes a means to distinctness. In Berg's mature works ultimately every phrase or partial entity not only divulges with complete clarity to cognitive understanding its formal function, but also makes that formal function so emphatic a part of the directly perceived phenomenon that a concluding phrase declares: I am a concluding phrase; and a continuation declares: I am a continuation. It is obvious that this unmistakable mastery of musical functions is a direct product of Berg's unquenchable longing for the amorphous and the formless, indeed, a direct product of the essence of his character. The statement that his pieces are polarized between extremes, each of which is mediated [*vermittelt*] by the other, refers not only to Berg's tone, to the expression and physiognomy of his works. It is a strict definition of their style [*Faktur*]. The style cannot withstand the reification of a musical entity [*das musikalische Etwas*], rather it must objectivize this primary response in order to give expression to it and thereby once again make nothingness into something [*Etwas*].

Analysis of Berg's music is legitimate because it is both possible and conceivable, which, to be sure, is the hidden basis for the whole idea of musical analysis: to grasp the artistic essence of music, its eloquence, its name, by way of technical facts. Berg's expression, that of a living organism maintaining itself by squandering itself, that of life as the essence of death, can be identified in the compositional aggregate. His music is without force, tangible and fatal like a vine; that comprises its true modernity, modernity of a kind that finds a genuine counterpart only in the properties of some exuberantly abstract creations of contemporary art and sculpture.

Alban Berg

From the analyses that follow, more still from the continuity of more than forty years' experience with Berg's music, such an agenda has emerged. What will be said about individual works can be little more than source material for those works, often vacillating between observations still indebted to an older form of analysis, and physiognomic descriptions focusing on the essential without translating it into technical detail sufficient to overcome the disparity between present musical understanding and Berg's creations. These creations sound moderately modern only so long as one remains ignorant of the paradox of a texture that is being simultaneously woven and unwoven with the same intricate care.

Piano Sonata

The Piano Sonata, Op. 1, is Berg's apprentice piece. Worked out to the last note, it can be proclaimed a complete success. But it bears the marks of the stress and agony of that achievement; the hand that conquered the recalcitrant material left its trace everywhere on the resultant form; to the experienced eye signs of its production are everywhere apparent in the product. If Anton Webern's lyrical genius manifests itself in complete, fully formed mastery in his first work, the Passacaglia, Berg's dynamic-dramatic genius insists on asserting *its* right to continuing development – and it is that development that prescribes the technological law governing each of his works. Precisely for that reason the Piano Sonata is ideally suited as an introduction to his music. As yet unconsolidated, it lies exposed before the listener; the urge to reconstruct its technical structure means in a certain sense to compose it a second time, out of itself; the piece is short, easily accessible, and not terribly difficult to perform; and thus reflection, in ready service to understanding, does well to linger here.

First of all, the work attests to the study of sonata form under Schoenberg's tutelage. One could well imagine that it came about in response to the assignment "sonata movement." For it is but *one* such movement; adding other movements is not necessary but certainly conceivable. Its didactic sonata simplicity remains unaffected by the principle of combining a number of movements into one, as is the case in Schoenberg's First Quartet and Chamber Symphony. On the other hand, the Sonata in all other respects is so completely indebted to the latter work that one can assert that Berg's stylistic development grew out of an insistent preoccupation with the compositional problems of the Chamber Symphony, whereas the older man had long since abandoned the iron closure of that procedure for new discoveries.

The debt owed the Chamber Symphony is acknowledged above all through the use of thematic reminiscences: the characteristic intervals of the beginning, for instance, the succession of perfect and augmented fourths, are found at the beginning of the [Chamber Symphony's] main theme (A D G #), and the sixteenth-note figure in the paradigm [*Modell*] of the secondary theme (Example 3, motive f) is borrowed almost literally from the close of the Chamber Symphony's transitional theme. More important is the identity of the proto-motivic "material": there are instances of whole-tone (cf. bars 8f.) and quartal (cf. bars 36ff.) formations, which, despite the work's fully developed though tonally interpreted chromaticism, are melodically and harmonically determinant.

Already, however, the central difference between Schoenberg's and Berg's treatment of the material is apparent. Fourths opened the Chamber Symphony: chordal in the introduction, melodic in the principal theme. They are expounded abruptly, with all the confidence of conquest. In Berg's Sonata, on the other hand, they first appear in bar 26 in an harmonically formative role. The quartal sonority F # −B−E is introduced in such a way that the critical note E appears as a suspension to D, that is, "harmonically foreign" to the tonic chord of the principal key of B minor, which, admittedly, is merely intimated. Imperceptibly, at first transposed down a fourth and initially immobilized and chromatically altered by a second voice, this quartal trichord gradually emancipates itself until finally revealed (bar 28) as a pure five-note quartal chord. However, with the help of a motivic remnant this chord is slowly altered, note by note, until (bar 29) it is transformed − once again as if at a border crossing − into an altered dominant of A major. That is how the quartal formation, at its appearance and disappearance, dissolves seamlessly into the tonal flow. It is this same tendency that leads Berg to reduce the self-assertive, fully graded fundamental intervals of the Chamber Symphony to unobtrusive, gliding, leading-tone relationships.

He adopts the new resources unconditionally and without ever depriving them, through facile play, of their formal function or formal claims. He does not combine them with traditional devices, but rather, as master of the smallest link, generates them therefrom; mediating not between styles, but between new and pre-existent resources; not as a cautious moderate or tempered modern − he was never that − but nevertheless always loyally safeguarding historical continuity, indeed, often as if reconstructing it. Schoenberg's discovery of quartal sonorities was utopian; Berg discovered them with memory's long, veiled gaze sunk into the past, that past which his music, even at its most daring, never forgets to consider. In this way the relationship between master and student continued, long after the student was himself a master.

Alban Berg

To be sure, the debt he owes Schoenberg in the Sonata goes incomparably deeper than in the conspicuously shared and already conspicuously modified musical material. It is the idea of the sonata itself, its exclusive, exhaustive motivic-thematic craftsmanship, which leaves nothing to chance and makes do with a minimum of given material: every theme in it is related to the principal theme (Example 1), though occasionally derived through multiple stages. Developing variation of the tersest "paradigms," association by means of motivic "remnants," derivation of all "accompaniments" out of thematic material − these serve as the most important means; all of them are prominently exemplified in the Chamber Symphony and with strict self-discipline translated by Berg into the more concise dimensions of the Sonata. Only a closer, though still much too fragmentary analysis of at least the exposition can furnish relevant insights.

Example 1

The Sonata's formal concept might be summed up as follows: within the smallest possible space an expansive profusion of thematic characters is derived from a minimum of motivic material; at the same time, the work is strictly unified in such a way that, despite its brevity, the abundance of shapes does not become confusing. This purpose is initially served by the construction of the principal theme (up to bar 11). It is clearly binary: a four-bar antecedent phrase which reaches a full cadence in the main key (cf. Example 1) − the whole phrase could be viewed as a single cadence − is followed by a longer, very modulatory consequent phrase, which does not sequence the antecedent phrase but rather extends it independently without actually having the effect of a contrasting idea. However, the motivic material of the consequent is derived entirely from the antecedent phrase; the novelty of its shape is the result of altered motivic succession. The antecedent phrase comprises three motives, which are mutually referential; (b) is an inversional, or even, if you will, retrograde-like variant of (a); (c) is derived from the rhythm and inversion of the minor second between the last note of (a), F♯, and the two first notes of (b), G. The consequent phrase now refers first to the later motivic segments (b) and (c), which, in close proximity, it immediately "adopts" as a remnant;

42

out of this remnant the concluding segment (c) is carried over through the fifth bar as a second remnant, in reiterated atomization of the material; only then does the terse opening motive (a) appear in transposition. But this motive in particular must not intrude as a repetition and is therefore − and this is extremely typical of the Sonata − restated in a manner midway between literal and "retrograde" repetition, which one might call "axis rotation"; the terse intervals are retained but their succession is altered; the three-note motive (a) begins with the second note, after which comes the first and then the third. Axis rotation is employed so consistently in the Sonata that it does not take much interpretive skill to see it as a prototype for the later serial technique; the motive is treated in the sense of a "basic idea" [*Grundgestalt*]. Its continuation is derived from sequences of the rhythmically compressed motive (b) in counterpoint with (c); Berg associates the two major thirds from (b) with the whole-tone chord; from that he melodically generates a descending whole-tone scale, which, in varied form, will have far-reaching consequences later (cf. Example 4, h). The first climax collapses with that scale; (b) and (c) fade away over pedals. The motivic segment (c) − a minor second and thus the smallest link *in nuce* − serves at the same time as an anticipation to the transitional theme.

The way Berg shapes the transition demonstrates his confident freedom in handling the schema [*Schema*] while remaining within that schema, in which the transition is assigned the function of "mediating" between the principal and secondary themes. Berg realizes that after such mediation, were it nothing but that, the extremely concise principal theme would be unable to hold its own in an extended exposition. On the other hand, one cannot simply dispense with mediation in a sonata so completely integrated motivically as this one. That is why transition and principal theme are combined in such a way that in retrospect the theme assumes a tripartite form. Initially, to be sure, the transition − already a contrast by virtue of its rapid tempo, and openly related to the principal theme only through motive (c) − commences as an entirely new variant of (a) (Example 2). Structurally, too, in contrast to the principal theme, the transition is laid out according to a one-bar "paradigm," which, rhythmically displaced,

Example 2

is imitated immediately at the distance of two quarter-beats; the added accompaniment in the upper voices is merely an augmented inversion of the paradigm. In bar 15 there is a standard sequence; the concluding segment of the paradigm is thereupon compressed and (bar 17) reinterpreted as the beginning of the re-entering principal theme, which, by means of motive (c), had during the preceding six bars been prepared and held fast, functioning as the anticipation for the transition. The principal theme's antecedent phrase returns melodically intact; its consequent phrase is interwoven with the conclusion of the antecedent in a rich contrapuntal combination and then spun out imitatively; the climax (bar 24) is marked by the entrance of that whole-tone succession from bar 8, in threefold augmentation and in counterpoint with repeated statements of the transition paradigm. The fourths passage follows, motivically derived from the inversion of the transition paradigm; the falling augmented fourth of the motive's conclusion is retained as a "remnant," varied with larger intervals, and then becomes, in its original form, the head motive of the secondary theme.

The secondary theme (bar 30) (Example 3), recognizable by the tender ninth chord with which it enters, is again structured on a paradigm, this time one that is two bars long. Its beginning is related to that of the principal theme by another "axis rotation": the intervals E−A#−B, starting with the last note and ascending directly, yield the principal theme's head motive: B−E−A# (= G−C−F#). The paradigm's second shape (Example 3, f) is a free variation of the diminution of motive (e). The first sequence (bar 32) employs a further axis rotation: D#−E−A from E−A−D#. Continuation of the secondary theme clearly shows the tendency toward rhythmic rejuvenation, utilizing for this purpose the sixteenths of motive (f).

Example 3

This rejuvenation induces a faster tempo: seamlessly, yet with vehemence, the closing theme appears at "veloce" [*rasch*] (bar 39). Its principal paradigm (Example 4) consists of the concluding [minor] second of (3f), the sixteenth sextuplets (4g), in which the rejuvenation culminates, and the melodic continuation (4h), which alludes to the whole-tone succession of bar 8 without adhering to its intervals. As at the augmentation

Piano Sonata

Example 4

of the whole-tone passage at bar 24, motive (4h) then leads to the now somewhat looser quartal harmony prepared by the dissolution of the E−A♭−D chord [bar 43] into E[♭]−A♭−D♭ [bar 44]. A long diminuendo, disrupted three times by the sextuplets, then complete resolution into whole-tone altered chords. These are retained, but only as accompaniment to a dark, broad *Abgesang* (bar 50, "viel langsamer") in which the agitated sextuplets settle into a melancholy calm. Quite literally *in*, for they *are* the *Abgesang*: the threefold augmentation of the concluding motive (4g). Of all the themes of the movement, this was the only one unrelated to the principal theme. That relationship, however, is established retroactively: by varying the intervals of the second bar of the *Abgesang*, which, as a "paradigm," is transformed into the beginning of the principal theme, thereby initiating the literal repetition − Berg employs repeat signs − of the principal section.

Brief comments must suffice for the remainder of the Sonata. Berg's infallible feeling for form is already evident in the disposition of the development section. After the combinatorial riches of the exposition it would be tautological and confusing to surpass its ingenuity with motivic and contrapuntal work. The governing principle of the development is exactly the opposite: the themes, once having passed through the discipline of the exposition, are allowed to breathe and sing out, just as the conclusion of the exposition had anticipated. In this way the development assumes an independent function, a function immediately promoted by the first developmental paradigm, a melodic combination of motive (a) with the descending whole-tone scale; the expressive gesture of the first bars of the development drifts by with the same deathly sorrow as later in the beginning of the big *Wozzeck* interlude, which appears to be dawning here even motivically. After this quiet episode the allegro character is re-established by the transition paradigm (2d), confronted now with a diminution of motive (b). This, in combination with motive (4h), achieves the grand climax, which, despite some imitation, is conceived homophonically and at one point sounds almost French in its harmonic style: made effective by means of the *simplification* of compositional texture. A caesura of the movement appears with a passage of pure fourths [bars 95f.], quite similar to the Chamber Symphony; it gives rise to a return that now joins motives (e) and (g), just as (b) and (h) had been coupled earlier; as it happens, the incipit of motive (4g) is the same as the conclusion of motive (f), which is in truth really motive (c). The reprise enters by way of the "smallest link."

The reprise [bars 110ff.] brings back all the important components of the exposition, though modified in the light of intervening events. Berg dispenses with a fusion of the principal and transitional themes. The principal theme has established itself firmly enough; while at the beginning of the Sonata it stood concisely self-contained as a motto, now, infused with the vitality of the development, it is propelled into the functional context. On the other hand, the ambiguous function of the transitional theme in the exposition needs clarification once and for all. That is why the reprise of the original principal theme is directly followed by the reprise of the developmental passage which in the exposition (bar 17) had grown from the transitional theme; only then, over six bars, is the actual transitional theme brought into play — conceptually a kind of double counterpoint of its original appearance, something like a fugal episode — together with a newly derived connective motive, an augmentation of (c). The secondary theme avoids recapitulatory inflexibility through variation of the opening interval. With compelling logic the concluding theme is further expanded out of the main development. The development section's decisive climax had employed motive (h), which is why it cannot just file past as if nothing had happened. After the return of the second quartal passage [bars 150f.] it is as if the music were remembering; with insatiable sequences of (h) it explodes in triple forte, only very gradually finding its way back into the prescribed course. But the *Abgesang*, expressing the definitive, returns confirmed; two bars literally repeated, two sequenced in the bass, then in inversion. Its "remnant" leads into the cadence: the first full cadence since the antecedent phrase of the principal theme. It clearly exhibits an inclination to present the melodic intervals of the head motive simultaneously as a sonority. In the melancholy of the conclusion there is once again a faint anticipation of serial technique.

Anyone who is serious about trying to understand Berg's music would do well to study thoroughly the eleven pages of this piano sonata. Beneath the thin, trembling hull of the outer form lies the entire dynamic power of this music, with all its technical correlatives; anyone capable of grasping its dialectic with the given constraints will not be swept into acoustical chaos later when, unfettered, it begets its true form out of itself.

Songs on texts by Hebbel and Mombert

After the demands his acute sense for form made in the Sonata upon his yearning for subjective expression, it is as if in the Four Songs, Op. 2, Berg let out a deep and exhausted sigh. Constructive multiplicity dissolves in the unity of captured "mood"; spontaneous wakefulness slips into the heavy drunkenness of sleep and dream; in place of tectonics the music gives itself entirely over unto itself. This developmental pattern recurred again and again with Berg: just as his feeling for life never quite lost its connection to the biological stratum; being able to breathe took on greater significance in his empirical existence than others can readily imagine. Everything that matters to him takes place between the extremes of expending himself and pausing [*Innehalten*].

Yet, the state of the subconscious into which the songs enter is an historical landscape; that of late- and neo-Romanticism. It fills Tristan's night with floating mists. The active, exacting ego, no longer able to master its alien world and almost never able to reach another state, is thrown back upon itself, loves itself in ecstasy and loathes itself unto death just as does that lost world; and, like the phantasmagoria of that world that it is, a vegetative soul, it thrives as in a hothouse: luxuriant illusion. In the songs more than anywhere else Berg approaches the addictive erotic loneliness of *Jugendstil*. To be sure, that loneliness is anything but alone; rather, it is a collective picture of its decade. Thus one can clearly hear reminiscences of Skryabin, and several bars at the end of the third song could, more primitively, be by Rudi Stephan, whom Berg surely knew as little as Stephan knew him. Loneliness as style is the loneliness one hears here.

Granted, more than just style. He who here "overcame the strongest of the giants" ["der Riesen stärksten überwand"], himself a giant, remained loyal to the illusion of dream and death without ever allowing himself to be deflected by optimistic slogans. But, like the giants, he transcended the illusion through his loyalty to it. The drowsiness of the songs, here still aesthetic "posture," is a look Berg's eyes never quite lost. Yet it is fundamental to the man. Whereas the songs are still safe in dalliance with their *monologue intérieur*, in *Wozzeck* this changes abruptly to real madness from oppression incarnate. There the substance of the songs is salvaged: in the three central chords of the scene in the field, in the chorus of the dreaming soldiers. Berg did not renounce the romantic past. He masters it through interpretation, by finally revealing its true [*scheinlos*] content as the anguish of estrangement [*Entfremdung*], a master of the smallest link with regard to content itself. Like heads and tails on a coin, Berg's music has two tendencies engraved one on each side: accurately to derive objective construction from subjective illusion, and: through construction to surpass the subjective essence. The crafty head and the trusty coat of arms are both engraved on Berg's coin and are in the end redeemed together at full value.

Not yet in the songs. The principles of the Lied are not wholly suited to Berg. Paradoxically enough: the technique of the smallest link is at odds with the small form. The integral is part of the differential; a single note or even mere tension can give rise to an opera or a symphony, but not to the static shape of an "inspired idea" as required by the dictates of the Lied. Berg knew very well why he wrote no more songs in his maturity; he objectified Lied impulses in large-scale forms such as the *Lyric Suite* and the aria *Der Wein.*

Thus the Songs, Op. 2, are more stylistic-historical documents of the development of that subjectivity which, breaking away and freeing itself from neoromantic ornamentation, leads to Expressionism in the strict sense: the last of the songs was published in the radical expressionist manifesto *Der blaue Reiter*, together with Schoenberg's *Herzgewächse* and Webern's "Ihr tratet zu dem Herde."

The compositional material is roughly analogous to that of the Sonata, but is treated homophonically throughout. Chromaticism, particularly altered dominant chords of all kinds, is even more prominent; also the interval of the major seventh, which − this may be the connection to Skryabin − is often introduced as an unresolved suspension to dominant ninth chords. Leading tones are employed everywhere as a symbol of the organic.

In the first song there is one palpable anticipation of *Wozzeck*; the compositional idea for the phrase "jener Wehen, die mich trafen" sketches the passage in *Wozzeck*, "der Mensch ist ein Abgrund." Despite all the chromaticism, the song is firmly established in the Schoenbergian sense of harmonic function [*Stufenbewußtsein*]. The assurance with which he shapes the final cadence is striking. In the second [song] a new method of inter-action becomes apparent: the technique of overlapping [*Verschränkung*], successfully employed in the relationship between voice and piano. The vocal line begins with a supple melody, accompanied, it would seem, purely chordally. In a lengthy interlude the piano picks up the "remnant" of the vocal theme and develops it imitatively. Cutting across this development is a new vocal entrance. However, it presents the initially obscured upper voice of the accompanimental chords, which thereby retroactively become thematic. The entire song grows out of the manipulation of those two themes. The third [song], short, concise and full of contrasts, is the piece about the giant; here one can already find signs of the eruptive power characteristic of Berg's mature music. At the same time it contains the antithesis of force: the first example of that letter symbolism to which Berg superstitiously adhered. The words "an einer weissen Märchenhand" are accompanied by a succession of notes A–B♭–B [German notation: A–B–H]: as initials of the names Alban/Berg/Helene.

The most important song of the group is the last. It no longer bears a key signature and represents Berg's first "atonal" composition. Not only is all reference to a central tonality abandoned, but even the construction of each of its wholly dissonant chords conspicuously avoids tonal implication. Nevertheless, dominant and leading-tone tendencies still predominate. The song's radicality does not reside in its harmonic language. Rather, it is in the *prose* with which Berg proceeds to demystify the pathos of the preceding songs, without relinquishing anything of their expressive power: the first stage toward *Wozzeck*. Berg was obviously influenced by Schoenberg's *Erwartung*, of which the text is reminiscent. The declamation is free of all symmetrical relationships, without, however, falling into recitative: the expressive urge invests even the asymmetrical melodies with perfect contour. As in its model *Erwartung*, the song largely dispenses with thematic work: no formal segment is repeated. The impulse that remained metaphorical in the other songs now becomes concrete: Berg's profound predisposition for the chaotic – source of all his skill in shoring up form – dares for the first time to reveal itself. This creates a real shock: a glissando passage, surely unprecedented in a song. In this moment of shock there is a flash of Berg's musical destiny: opera. The glissando is an operatic gesture. The low B♭ is likewise operatic, a percussion effect, which in the song seems to take up much too much time. The transgression here against form is of the kind demanded by opera, which as a form remains so dreadfully difficult and unsecured because its formal precepts command – for their fulfillment – their own transgression. Later, Berg's formal instinct for opera was never more splendidly triumphant than when the *constructeur* extricates himself from the construction; where the operatic form reflects upon itself through a consoling pause. Thus Wozzeck asks what time it is. That may be the secret of the pause represented by the songs, the last of which is perhaps the only thoroughly anarchic work Berg ever wrote. But its anarchy contains the cipher of its order.

Seven Early Songs

This is the place to speak of the Seven Early Songs, which are somewhat peripheral to Berg's oeuvre. They were written around 1907, in other words before the Piano Sonata, but not orchestrated until 1928, the year both

Alban Berg

the original and orchestral versions were published. They belong to different stylistic and material spheres. Some, like the enraptured "Nachtigall," refer unabashedly back to the high Romanticism of Schumann and Brahms; "Liebesode" is already touched by the heavy perfume of Opus 2; "Nacht" speaks the idiom of Impressionism; "Sommertage," and even more the setting of the Rilke poem, "Das war der Tag der weissen Chrysanthemen," seem, in their confrontation with Schoenberg's Chamber Symphony, like greatly advanced preliminary studies to the Sonata. Negligible as the difficulties are in understanding songs of this nature, it is all the more difficult – precisely because of their nature – to understand their publication. They are therefore more in need of apologia than of commentary.

The objections are twofold. On the one hand one asks why the mature Berg even published a work so clearly outside his true "style." That can be countered by arguing that it is inappropriate to apply the historical concept of style directly as a critical concept. Let those smugly triumph over the dependencies of the songs who, schooled on the classic and romantic, apply their modest stylistic categories as ready clichés that allow them their officious categorizations; and those who thereby consider themselves exempted from the need to consider style itself as a dialectical whole consisting of a tension between creative musical power and the "creative conditions," namely the musical language [*Material*] at hand. However, those who take that trouble will be rewarded not just with beauty. They will recognize how in the middle section of "Nachtigall" – to start with the most objectionable song – there is a gentle force to the tone that the conventional means cannot conceal, can, indeed, hardly encompass; just as in the dim light of "Schilflied" there is already a glimmer of the light that glows like an eternal solar eclipse in the field and streets of *Wozzeck*; how nobly in "Traumgekrönt" that I craves happiness, still trusting in fulfillment, before sinking into the poetry of sleep and death as into a land in which that dreamed-of someone no longer enters "sweetly and softly" [*"lieb und leise"*].

Of course cleverer individuals can see that all of the above constitutes the second, the denunciatory objection: the songs and their musical language are Berg's original and true nature, which, in bondage to his teacher's demonic spell, he then deflected and intellectually falsified. To begin with, if Berg's mature style is supposed to confute the early work, then the early work should make the later suspect. But that is to ignore the fact that the teacher's demonic spell was one devoted to truth and therefore not demonic: musical language itself is not substance, and the first is not the original and certainly not the true nature. Rather, musical language is secondary nature, from which freedom must first be won; that which is given is historical material [*Stoff*], in which creative power takes an inventive hand while following its dictates; so it is not creative power at all, but that which confronts it and only through resistance helps create it.

One can counter: that that musical language is actually one fundamentally suited to Berg, as demonstrated by the fact that it continually returns in his oeuvre: the F minor of the Bible scene, the D minor of the big interlude in *Wozzeck* being drastic examples of a universal tendency.

There is no need to dispute that the delayed publication of the Early Songs is related to the stubborn return in Berg's developed style of elements of his initial, precritical language. But far from compromising the stylistic purity of *Wozzeck*, this delayed orchestration actually contributes to one's understanding of its meaning. When it was said that Berg, doggedly faithful, revealed through construction the illusion of the subjective-romantic essence and transformed it by means of that revelation, this was not the formulation of an *aperçu* alien to the language, but rather a statement of fact that can be technically elaborated.

For Berg's loyalty to illusion resides not only in the fact that he did not disavow the Early Songs, or that he divulged the blushing music of a youth without blushing. Rather, loyalty is seen in the orchestration itself. The orchestration adheres to even the smallest compositional details of the songs, so as to make them clear and transparent; it works the songs out fully, even their illusion. Yet, through its very loyalty the orchestration stands in contradiction to the invoked romantic essence to which it remains loyal. It was never the goal of romantic, at least of post-Wagnerian orchestration, to give clear articulation to construction, but rather to ornament and obscure it. Berg, however, aims so passionately for the objective derivation of sound out of composition that the orchestral version of these romantic songs can be considered quite simply the prototype of his new constructive orchestrational style and can enhance our understanding of that style in the same way the Piano Sonata did with regard to his motivic technique.

The central principle of Berg's motivic technique, that of unconditional continuity, applies to the orchestration as well. Its goal is that music and sound be mutually indifferent; not indifferent sound, as in the neoclassical composers' rigid treatment of winds and terrace dynamics, but rather in the sense of identity. Sound is made responsible for the entire range of the music's differentiation, and sound serves that task by means of incessant, dynamic inflection. However, the functional principle of such continual fluctuation is that the sounds change by preserving elements of the preceding sound – of preceding instruments or groups – as "remnants" to be incorporated in the subsequent sound, so that the new, varied sound develops imperceptibly out of the preceding one. In the fifth bar of the first song, for instance, a new thematic character enters the composition as an inconspicuous accompanimental voice, a sixteenth-note figure, initially introduced by the first violins, then imitated by the woodwinds, and leading to the actual commencement of activity, the main section in A major. The new thematic character succeeds in recoloring the entire orchestration. The whole-tone chords in eighth-notes, which originally belonged to the woodwinds, are transferred − with a slight increase in motivic activity leading to a gradual melting of the dark inflexibility of the beginning − to the warmer tone of the horns; at the same time the horns continue the clarinet's legato while slowly, step by tiny step, modifying the sound; meanwhile the same string pizzicati that from the beginning had doubled the woodwind eighths serve as a connective "remnant." That is how faithfully the orchestration follows the compositional course throughout.

But that alters the composition. Perhaps most strikingly at the end of the first song. The piano version is in straightforward tripartite form: its end merges with the beginning. The orchestration, however, is able to reinterpret the repetition in light of the intervening events as completely as the reprise of the Piano Sonata had reinterpreted its exposition through motivic work. To be sure, deep woodwinds and pizzicati are again combined to establish the reprise as such in terms of sound, too; but the strings, set free in the middle section, are not just allowed to disappear again: the flow of time is not simply reversible. Their eloquent tone is still present where the music is already entirely identical with the beginning. Combining familiar with newly acquired material, the orchestration works out a temporal course of events that had been latent in the song's piano version. After the dynamic middle section static repetition would have been inappropriate.

But such constructive modifications, which follow the music's own compositional demands, ultimately suspend that music's romantic "style." First through critique of the tutti sound, which in the romantic orchestra invariably attempts to gather all refractions in the harmonic/melodic texture to an unrefracted whole and to relate every detail to a fictitious infinity − that of the open horizon of the string tutti perspective. Berg no longer permits such a fiction; individual events have their individual sound without concern for a preconceived totality; where there is a total sound it is compelled by the events themselves − that is, by the musical design. That further means: desubstantialization of the sound. Out of the necessity of the piano accompaniment he makes the virtue of an almost incorporeal orchestra, one that never inflates and is never larger or more pretentious than the music; just clear and euphonious, in keeping with the function and

First String Quartet

perfectly fitted to the body of the music. The orchestration was done during the time of *Lulu*; with the same stubborn insistence which in the last opera masterfully makes even illusion thematic as a colorful world of illusion, along with loyalty to that illusion, the orchestration succeeds in making illusion the object of construction.

To be sure, it is only possible for such construction to come to grips with the illusoriness of the Early Songs after having already prevailed over language more truly [*scheinlos*] appropriate to it; possible only in *self-conscious awareness* of the illusion, not in naive execution. That is why the songs were only orchestrated in ripe maturity. Berg resolved them in the true Hegelian double sense: to destroy and salvage. The enigmatic image of this strange cycle embraces an historical process as its content. But that process is nothing other than a playful paradigm for Berg's entire history.

First String Quartet

Berg liked to say that he wrote the String Quartet, Op. 3, in defiance, after a publishing firm turned down the Piano Sonata. But the gesture of haughty self-assertion with which the piece begins and ends is that of a breakthrough. With abrupt, violent exertion it seizes full mastery; fitfully exhaling, the master proclaims himself. Nothing remains of the apprentice's self-consciousness, nothing of the emotional decor of *Jugendstil*; while the Quartet's sorrow and passion are those of real life and not merely ornamental anticipation of these emotions, the technical resources of the Piano Sonata are now set free within the scope of a grand design.

There is scarcely a more original design in all of Berg. If any of his works warrants reassessment, then it is the Quartet that even today cries out for correct interpretation to rescue it from the shadow cast by the success of the *Lyric Suite*. Whatever edge the forty-year-old [composer] may have over the twenty-five-year-old in terms of objective experience and command is offset by the reckless immediacy, highly aggressive, elemental force of the latter's focused subjectivity; there are very few early works of this kind in music history. Naturally, it has its stylistic precursors, like any other work. Schoenberg's F♯ minor Quartet is the most readily apparent: the closing theme group of the first movement, for instance (bar 58), is reminiscent of an important motive from Schoenberg's work, and is also treated similarly. But the similarities never go beyond those of detail. The invention and execution are wholly Berg's; no model can be found.

Berg's invention is the spontaneous correlate of his grasp of the fact that the principle of differentiation and large instrumental form belong together. At a time when Schoenberg and Webern had set that question

53

aside, either contracting the temporal dimension or wedding its articulation to the poetic word, Berg, following the impulse of his creative strength – which he himself understood to be architectonic – never lost sight of the totality of the musical whole, even while remaining aware of music's unrepeatable irretrievability. In lone anticipation, the First Quartet manifests a formative will that only many years later asserted itself across the spectrum of progressive music. That same will was also present in Reger. But Berg applies it in an incomparably more advanced way – not obediently accepting the large forms handed down by tradition, not filling old skins with new wine, not using chromaticism and enharmonicism to give modernistic enrichment to the unexamined schemata of the sonata, variation, and rondo; rather, from the very beginning he displays the resolve to produce large forms rigorously and with originality out of the motivic/ thematic principles of construction worked out by Schoenberg and adapted in the Piano Sonata. It is a confirmation of both the consistency of Schoenberg's subsequent stylistic development and of the young Berg's perspicacity that the Quartet, especially in the second movement, already quite clearly demonstrates procedures that later, elevated to a norm, are called the twelve-tone method.

Yet he would not be the master of utmost caution had he pursued his predilection for large forms other than with keen awareness of contemporary approaches to the formal problem. What marks the Quartet as a work of genuinely dialectical character is the fact that its architecture emerges from a loyal critique of the architecture that had until then been requisite for chamber music. While Reger used this as a dependable hull, believing that he could infuse his intentions into it without contradiction, Berg met not only the authentic requirements of the form, but also those of his own explosive impulses, and to the end maintained the conflict between them. Not a single element remains that does not receive its rationale entirely from its relationship to the formal whole – and, though formal abstractions do not precede "inspiration," there is likewise no form not legitimized by the requirements and impulse of the individual elements. What results from the conflict, however, is nothing less than the *liquidation of the sonata*. The essence of sonata form is at the heart of the Quartet; it disintegrates under the assault of unfettered, subjectively musical creativity; its disintegration, however, liberates the objective forces within it, permitting the creation of a new symphonic form in free atonality.

Understanding the dialectical disposition of the Quartet leads to a recognition of its difficulty, which must be kept in mind if it is to be dealt with properly. It is indeed extraordinarily difficult; that alone explains why this quartet's exemplary achievement has been so insufficiently acknowledged in performance. The difficulty lies first of all in the depreciation of the individual element through the whole created by the formal dialectic. The Quartet no longer has any "themes" in the old static sense, at least not in the second movement. Permanent transition softens every consolidated shape, opening it to what precedes and follows, holding it in a never-ending flow of variants, subordinating it to the primacy of the whole. Thematic paradigms shrivel: they are reduced to minimal motivic units. If in the case of the Piano Sonata the themes were fragmented into such units through "elaboration," the academic difference between inspiration and elaboration now disintegrates before a master's critique: both converge. Inspiration becomes a function of the whole, while the whole becomes the aggregate of motivic fragmentation. The listener's task is therefore not that of noting themes and following their fate, but that of becoming involved in a musical process in which every bar, indeed, every note is equidistant to the center. That kind of difficulty is more concretely one of material disposition itself. The dominant material principle remains the chromatic step. It governs the melodic substance of the work, which, throughout, either rejuvenates itself in the half-step interval or expands into the half-step interval. But the accompanying harmony is no longer one of dominants. It is largely emancipated and results from counterpoint and motivic construction: in other words, it no longer offers the surface coherence still preserved in the Piano Sonata. The unity of horizontal and vertical dimensions in the later twelve-tone technique is anticipated in the Quartet by chromatic "twelve-tone-ness." The ear can therefore depend neither on a line whose traditional accompaniment glides by familiar and unnoticed, nor on expressive harmonic values, such as earlier assert themselves in the songs. Instead, one must listen with comprehensive attentiveness in order to slash one's way through the Quartet's vegetative impenetrability. This is as true for the single element as for its dialectical counterpart, the formal whole. Granted, once again both movements preserve formal paradigms − that of the sonata in the narrow sense and that of the sonata rondo. But the developmental principle has so completely absorbed them that an understanding of the traditional form can no longer contribute anything to an understanding of the actual process. Decisive is not what remains of the sonata form, but what has been changed; it is of no use to know when in the Quartet the secondary theme, closing theme, or rondo reprise began, but rather what unique purpose each unique event fulfills.

Nevertheless, the sonata schema is still clearly apparent in the first movement. It is wedded to the idea of a slow movement, whose inconsolable melancholy gravitates toward immersion in the form. But this form is viewed critically throughout. The understanding at work in the Piano Sonata necessitates taking the next step. In the Sonata, the transitional theme was joined with the principal theme in tripartite fashion. Now, the transitional theme is swept aside: everything and nothing is transition. On the other hand, the principal thematic complex itself is based upon two contrasting, yet mutually derivable motives, which over the course of forty bars undergo the most varied combinatorial development. The actual secondary theme (bar 48) is preceded by a very brief introduction (bar 41), which refers back to the motivic material of the principal thematic complex, becoming heir, as it were, to the function of a transitional theme, while at the same time (cf. bars 52f.) influencing the secondary theme itself and thus unifying both thematic groups. The concluding theme (bar 58) enters in sharp contrast, but immediately disappears in the texture. The tendency toward liquidation of the sonata is most clearly apparent in the development (bars 81 – 104). While the consistently developmental character of Op. 1 led inevitably to a simplification of the actual development section, it now requires its contraction: between eighty bars each of exposition and reprise the development section is now granted only twenty bars. The core of the sonata shrivels at the same time that its driving force permeates its farthest extremities. Thus the schema is suspended: later, the first movement of the *Lyric Suite* is a sonata without a development section. The development section of the Quartet's first movement uses as paradigm only the concluding motive and a motive from the second theme, carefully bypassing the principal thematic material; as if it were merely a coda to the second theme complex. The development of the first [theme complex] is transferred to the intruding, varied reprise.

Example 5

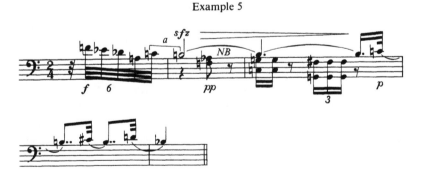

The piece begins with a supple main motive in thirty-second sextuplets (Example 5), whose remnant (5a), the half-step, is retained and varied through chromatic interval expansion; in the fourth bar an imitative answer to it in the viola. A three-bar consequent phrase in the first violin (Example 6), employing the derived interval of a major third,

Example 6

and at the same time anticipating principal motives of the second theme group; in fact, the Quartet generally combines the technique of "remnants" with one of anticipation. In the tenth bar the contrasting idea enters, somewhat faster (Example 7), and is immediately combined contrapuntally with the main motive in the cello (5). Its rhythm is from the consequent phrase (6), but its melodic core (7b) is derived in a fashion which, as an anticipation of row technique, deserves attention. The accented note B of the main motive (5) together with the first two notes of the accompanying

Example 7

line in the viola constitute the row B−A♭−G (cf. Example 5, NB). But the transposed retrograde of this row is motive (7b): E−F−A♭. The vertical dimension is thus dissected. The whole of the expansive first theme group from bar 14 on is derived from the basic material thus introduced; the intervallic expansion in the conclusion of Example (5) and the inversion of the motivic core (7b) play a significant role here. Build-up to a climax in bar 28: the main motive (5) in the upper violin range, accompanied by (7b) reduced to sixteenth triplets. Triple forte, imitation of the main motive in all instruments. Diminuendo with intervallic expansion of Example (5), the consequent phrase (6) coda-like in the cello (bars 36ff.). Complete silence.

Introduction to the second theme group: initially idle accompaniment, then a violin motive (bar 43), which appears to be an axis turn of (7b), but actually anticipates the later (8d). Cello recitative (bar 45), citing the consequent phrase (6), which is also still present in the second theme (cf. Example 8f). The second theme begins *a tempo* and closely joins four contrasting motives together (8). The opening motive (8c) is closely related to the conclusion of (6); (8d) is a variant of (8c); the only completely "new"

Alban Berg

element in the whole complex is the terse segment (8e). That is spun out, but already after four bars the paradigm of the concluding thematic group (bars 58–61) appears in pure intentional [*ausgehörter*] atonality.

Example 8

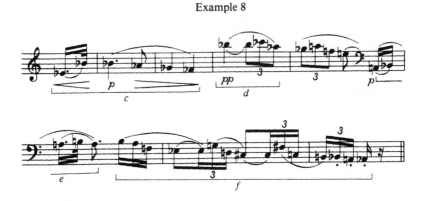

Development of this paradigm is dispensed with; initially it is no more than an interpolation in the second theme. The motives of Example (8) are immediately resumed and calmly developed by means of combinatoriality and retrograde. Only toward the close of the section (as of bar 77) is a thirty-second note figure from the accompaniment of the secondary theme, originally related to (8c), transformed into the accompaniment of the concluding paradigm.

This figure, accompanied by flageolet chords, introduces the development (bar 81). A recitative-like continuation in the viola, which relates the concluding paradigm to (8f). Six bars of elaborate polyphonic treatment of the closing paradigm and its retrograde. Simplification as of bar 90: entrance of motive (8e) from the second theme, related to the preceding material through a dotted rhythm. After five bars, resumption of the concluding paradigm, now combined with (8e). As accompaniment to the concluding paradigm and in quadruple forte the main voice brings a motive related to (8f) and the consequent phrase (6). Completely seamless return to the beginning, in which the perfect fourth from the concluding figure in thirty-seconds is linked with the descending fourths of the cello's accompaniment to the main theme (5).

In strict economy the reprise (bar 105) restricts itself to the given motivic material, but varies the succession to such an extent as to avoid all repetition of the unrepeatable – thereby, however, abandoning the schematic tripartite nature of sonata form. The main motive remains firmly on the accented B. Initially Berg foregoes the intervallic expansion. Instead, an independent march-like pattern is created (as of bar 108) from the accompanimental rhythm of the beginning, and that is combined with development of the idea of the consequent phrase (6) (i.e., the introductory recitative to the second theme). Only at the conclusion of the section is the intervallic expansion recalled. Bar 119 − corresponding to bar 10 − hooks up with the contrasting idea of the principal theme group (7b). A kind of second strophe is fashioned out of its inversion (bars 126ff.), later with a continuing contrapuntalization of the main theme (5). This strophe acquires unmistakable transitional character; toward the end it develops imitatively the idea of motivic [intervallic] expansion from (5) and without break or introduction connects the main thematic group to the second theme. The reprise of that second theme (as of bar 138) completely transforms the sonata schema. Leaving out the initial segments, it restricts itself to (8e) and (8f), but expands them to a second development section in the highest string register; first canonically, then using (8e) and (8f) in sixteenth triplets as accompaniment to their own original shape. As of bar 149 the passage dies away with the original counterpoint to (8c) as the principal voice.

Only then a real caesura. The last section, beginning in bar 153, could only superficially be explained by sonata terminology. In accordance with the dictates of the sonata this section makes good the reprise of themes held in abeyance until then − above all (8c) and the concluding paradigm; however, the structural function is that of an extended coda. It is dominated by the first theme, whose accompaniment again begins as a march; the main motive (5) and the concluding phrase (6) follow (bar 157). Resumption of the reprise: in bar 159 the concluding paradigm enters as an interpolation (corresponding to bar 58), followed by the repetition of (8c). Coda weariness causes the music to sink toward the conclusion of the movement by means of harmonic leading tones. (8c) leads (as of bar 169) into an augmentation of the main motive (5); thereupon that motive is revealed in its original thirty-second sextuplet form. As of bar 177 the concluding paradigm constitutes a recognizable concluding group, but already after three bars (bar 180) the augmented main motive (5), in counterpoint with (7b), pushes to the fore. A splintering into remnants until the end: the main motive (5) over the original accompanying harmonies.

The second movement, of symphonic allegro character despite many slow interjections, manipulates the rondo form in such a way that, though the − very concise − principal theme is repeated in a refrain-like manner between the various sections, it is so thoroughly varied that it scarcely appears as a "theme" but merely supplies raw material, just as in the case of a row: the rondo is transformed into free prose. Thematic relationships are complicated by the fact that the themes refer back to those of the first movement; there are occasional quotations from that movement, though generally in the form of variants and derivations. It could be roughly schematicized as follows: first thematic complex up to bar 47; first rondo reprise as of bar 48; second theme-like group and transition from bars 54 to 71; development with multiple rondo entrances as of bar 72; reprise bar 151. More fruitful is a look, however brief, at the musical events themselves.

Vehement, jagged entrance of the principal theme (Example 9): open eruption of the expressionistic Berg. The theme takes determined hold of

Example 9

the motive (9h), a reminiscence of the intervallic expansion of the first movement. Added to that, in the second violin's tremolo at the bridge, the counterpoint (9i): anticipation of the striking contrasting idea (10), which follows immediately, succeeded by (9h) and then (bar 8) the retrograde of the conclusion of (10): continuing effects of the stentato characteristics of (9h), which permeate the entire movement. At bar 10 the first variant of the principal theme (9g) in the viola: augmented and with a new rhythm.

Example 10

This is developed and rejuvenated through another variant of the three concluding notes of (9g). That variant prepares for the diminution of the contrasting idea (10) (bar 22). Its sharp definition, too, falls prey to the musical flow; it is joined (bar 25) by a variant that includes the rhythm of the main motive (5) from the first movement (Example 11). Row-like development of (10). Presto plunging descent, checked on chords that permeate the movement as signature harmonies (Example 12). Transition-like passage, created from a fresh variant of (10) (grazioso, bar 39) and (11). Bar 48 rondo entrance of the theme in diminution (9g);

Example 11

Example 12

Example 13

development of one of its motivic segments. Hint of a second theme as of bar 55, deliberately less supple than the principal themes, related to (9) as well as to the principal secondary theme (8c) and (8d). Another rondo entrance (cello, bars 60f.), transition by means of the stentato idea.

A long, very segmented developmental section as of bar 72. Initially using a paradigm from the second theme (Example (13); related to (8c)). Thereupon the grazioso variant of (10) (from bar 39) joins in and disappears in an imitative accompanimental passage (as of bar 80); continuing adherence to the stentato idea. Renewed rondo entrance of (9g) (bar 88), presto unison, with totally new rhythm taken up by the signature chords (12) (bar 91). Their minor second interval is developed; strophic repetition of the rondo entrance of bar 88 (bar 103), only now (9g) in close counterpoint and related to (10). As of bar 119 a quiet, structurally independent episode; its paradigm (in the second violin) is a combination of the last segment of (11) with a motive from the first thematic complex (bars 13f.). As of bar 133 inversion of the episodic paradigm. Return using (9g) and the inversion of the grazioso variant of (10); extreme stentato effect.

The principal theme (9g) in its original violin register (bar 151) marks the beginning of the reprise, which is treated with total freedom, wholly as prose. The contrasting ideas (9) and (10) diverge sharply. The principal theme of the first movement is incorporated into (9) (bar 168), its contours thereupon dissolved in the accompanimental harmonies. These are imperceptibly transformed into the signature harmonies (12) and form – always with reference to the first movement – an accompaniment to (10) (bar 181). Transition, again using (11) and the grazioso variant of (10). The second theme (bar 200), kept carefully in the background in the exposition, now advances to the fore, with the effect – critique of the sonata form! – of being new; but soon (as of bar 209) it is deflected back into (10) and from there into the coda. Collapse over the motive (12), standstill. Dramatic gesture of the conclusion: bar 223 last rondo entrance of (9g), one last appearance of the main motive (5) from the first movement. The relationship of (9h) to the intervallic expansion of (5) is revealed and the stentato heightened to orchestral dimensions. Ecstatic arrogant gesture in conclusion.

The Altenberg Songs

The *Five Orchestral Songs on Picture Postcard Texts of Peter Altenberg*, Op. 4, written in 1912, were discussed by Ernst Krenek in the 1937 Berg book. Even today his contribution is eminently worth reading, as much for his spontaneously conveyed familiarity with the compositions, as for modifications, which recent performances of the rediscovered songs have made necessary. Should one be searching for drastic proof of the hypothesis that, over time, music changes within itself, then one need look no further than this Op. 4. It is not to diminish its brilliance to point out that the shock value that led to a scandal at the premiere, which Krenek still stressed, dissipated in the years following Berg's death, as was the case, incidentally, with Krenek's own youthful compositions. On the other hand, the "tinge of classicism" to which, as a true authority, he likewise drew attention, has been confirmed. In a Hessian Radio performance of May 1967, in which Michael Gielen and Heather Harper included the songs in a program of later composers, they had as compelling an effect as Webern pieces have in the company of music composed after 1945. Surely the primary reason for that is their sound. It is scarcely conceivable that in his first orchestral work – in other words, in the absence of everything that goes by the fatal compliment of routine – a composer could achieve such perfection and balance of sensuous phenomena; extravagances once considered notorious were even then integrated effortlessly into the surface. Krenek pointed out the "destruction of ordered tonal boundaries" through glissandi in the trombone or in string harmonics and the technique (subsequently exploited by Bartók) of lowering the pitch of the timpani during a roll – these things

The Altenberg Songs

later inspired the description of various idiosyncrasies of Leverkühn's style in *Doktor Faustus*; amazing the extent to which all of these things are today integrated into the whole, how little anything sticks out. Cocteau's maxim, that an artist must know how far to go too far is confirmed by the huge orchestra of these miniatures. That is due principally to the extraordinary precision of [Berg's] instrumental imagination. There is not one timbral combination in the score, no matter how exposed, that did not pass through his inner ear; nowhere does experimentation reach the point where the sound eludes compositional control. If contemporary composers frequently reject that approach, it is not always because they have advanced beyond it, but rather because their technical abilities are often not up to the demands of such control: loosening that control was legitimate only where it could be perceived as having been once present and then negated.

The songs likewise profit from a procedure one could call the technique of [dissonance] preparation. Just as under the rules of strict sixteenth-century counterpoint dissonances were allowed only under very specific circumstances (all related − subject to the primacy of the pure triad − to the nature of their entrance), in this phase of Berg's work the sonoral dissonances and, to a certain extent, by analogy the harmonic dissonances, are subject to similar constraints. To be sure, even then he did not shy from excessive combinations of any kind, but motivated each and every one. Nothing is simply set down, everything is derived, as if the moment in which an aesthetic phenomenon occurs − that moment being critical to aesthetic stylization in general − were cause for unsurmountable difficulties. The only match for these difficulties is a circumspection equal to the excess. Proust's prose experienced the same difficulty; today it has reached a point where any expression of the aesthetic, the fictitious has become difficult. In the Altenberg Songs Berg's circumspection also transfers to the sonoral dimension the primacy of *becoming* over *being*. Colors are not just painted in as if pre-existent, they are developed; the process by which they are created becomes their justification. Thus the conclusion of the first song is defined by a sustained chord in the harmonium, E−B−F, which already lay concealed in the piano in bar 1 and then moved upward chromatically. One could point to models in Schoenberg works from approximately the same period. But the chord enters inaudibly in the third section amid a tutti fortissimo and is only thrown into relief through subtraction, through the extinguishing of all other articulated events. That way it establishes itself as something that has been there all along. In the Altenberg Songs the most delicate discretion is tantamount to audacity.

It would be appropriate to Berg to consider the proportional balance of the songs in conjunction with the form of the entire cycle; this micrological composer placed the greatest importance on macro-structure.

The design of the whole, as in sonata-like form, is held together by two rather extended and above all dynamically expansive movements at the beginning and end; there are parallels in early Webern, just as in some respects, of all the works in Berg's oeuvre, the Altenberg Songs most closely approximate the techniques of his friend.

In a rudimentary fashion the first piece follows a formal principle Berg was to use frequently thereafter: gradually, with concurrent dynamic build-up, compositions are led from the amorphous to the articulate and then, occasionally with acts of destruction, back into the indeterminate. More than any other kind of row manipulation, this procedure contains teleologically within it the idea of the retrograde, little though the third section of that song can in fact be considered a true retrograde reprise. – The last song is a passacaglia and, like "Nacht" of *Pierrot lunaire*, expressly proclaims itself as such. This fixed form, which Schoenberg and Berg chose freely, induces in both composition and texture more cohesive, less disintegrated, indeed, more familiar design. That is the source of that unifying force, ever the goal of new music, which is fundamentally open-ended. Though the problem of closure can never be completely solved, it can nowhere be ignored. The price the passacaglia must pay is its subtle stylistic divergence from the other songs, somewhat analogous to the relationship of the last song of Webern's Op. 3 to the preceding ones. The three middle [Altenberg] pieces are far shorter than the outer songs.

Thirty years later the "chaos" of the long instrumental introduction of the first song, to which Krenek drew attention – it is as if its expanse were meant to justify the extraordinary profusion of orchestral devices – no longer exists. It proves to be gradually expanding but sustained ostinato complexes differing metrically in the vertical dimension and not coinciding with the bar lines. As of the ninth bar expressive melodic beginnings become noticeable. The similarity of the idea behind the sonoral design with that of the opening to the prelude of Schreker's *Gezeichneten* is striking, except that Berg's work, surely written earlier, goes much further in its use of dissonance than Schreker with his polytonally clouded triads; seldom, however, is a certain affinity between the two as palpable as it is here.[1] The differences are all the more relevant. Here as there it is a case of mixed sonority [*Mischklang*]. Schreker's sound virtually eradicates the individual colors in its shimmering totality, they are perceptible only as momentary reflexes within a homogeneous sound. The nature of Berg's mixed sonority, on the other hand, which is indebted to the color piece in Schoenberg's Op. 16, is such that while the simultaneously juxtaposed colors likewise

---

1 Nor is there a lack of structural cross-connections with Schreker. In the big duet passages between Alwa and Lulu many motivic complexes return almost insatiably (sameness in the midst of diversity); similarly in the atelier scene of the *Gezeichneten*.

blend into a whole, they at the same time remain unhomogeneous, independently layered: mixed sound without mixture. It is no mere analogy to periods in painting to call Schreker's technique late-impressionistic, Berg's early-expressionistic. The introduction to the first Altenberg Song is far more profoundly infused with the idea of chamber music than is Schreker's conception, in which, according to Schreker himself, the orchestra is to sound like a single instrument. By contrast, Berg's compositional approach and overall technique exhibit, at least in his earlier works, a decided tendency toward the dissociative, extending even to his instrumentation. His sound, like his motivic-thematic organization, yearns to return to its component elements. Planned disorganization becomes organization; such clear-cut intention transforms those eighteen instrumental bars into something other than the chaos they initially appeared to be.

In light of developments in music since 1945, the entrance of the voice deserves particular attention. The first note is produced with gently closed lips, the second with half-open mouth, "wie ein Hauch an- und abzusetzen" [begin and end like a breath of air]; only the third [note], accompanying the first word of text, is sung in the usual manner: rudimentary, three-tiered *Klangfarben* row, anticipating the subsequent incorporation of the parameter of color into serial technique. The color row is motivated by the principle of the differential. Since Berg seems almost embarrassed to allow the voice to begin – as if song should not become audible with so little effort – he must invoke it as if out of a pre-musical realm. This, in turn, cannot be done with force; rather, involuntary continuity with the artificial must be preserved. Of the trends that later converge in twelve-tone and serial techniques, this one is particular to Berg; already in the opening of the Orchestral Pieces, Op. 6, he employs it emphatically as an artistic technique. His way of composing takes as its rule: *musica non facit saltus*; that gives rise in all dimensions to successions of interlocking individual events. Leaving aside for the moment the principle of infinitesimalism, the natural result is quasi-serialism. Kolisch noticed the same phenomenon when dealing with *Klangfarben* in his analysis of Berg's string technique in the Allegro misterioso of the *Lyric Suite*.

The three middle songs are likewise architecturally related to one another. Apart from the fermata on a chord at midpoint, the extremely short "Sahst du nach dem Gewitterregen" can dispense with obvious segmentation; however, in bar 8 a motive from the second bar is taken up by the voice and imitated by the cellos, thereby producing a rudimentary reprise effect; the closing F of the solo contrabasses, too, is reminiscent of the F with which the instrumental accompaniment begins in the second bar. The overall design of the song is that of tying a knot, paralleling Webern's technique during those same years. In the fifth bar the voice departs from Wagner's

Alban Berg

dictates of natural declamation with a coloratura-like melisma; there was nothing like it again until Boulez's *Marteau sans maître*.

Berg's sense of form answers this song in the next one, the third, with a somewhat denser texture within the smallest possible space. The twelve-tone complexes at the beginning and end have become famous. Instrumentally the accompaniment in the extremely terse middle section is created out of a remnant, the [falling] sixth in an oboe melody. The conclusion's quasi-melodic dissection of the twelve-tone-like opening harmony fixes upon a crucial aspect of twelve-tone technique, namely, upon the equivalence of vertical and horizontal. And yet, from the standpoint of advanced twelve-tone technique, the procedure here is quite simple, just as in general the songs' compositional texture – in contrast to the principal event, the orchestration – is marked by a certain simplicity. However, one should not therefore hasten to proclaim the third song an early precursor of twelve-tone composition. Even after he wrote in a strictly consistent twelve-tone style, Berg was never particularly interested in the refinements inherent to the serial method. Occasionally, as in the *Lyric Suite*, he was accused of twelve-tone primitivism. Unjustly. For while Berg, particularly Berg the dramatist, intended to use the twelve-tone technique to organize the raw material, he also worked at maintaining sufficient latitude so as to adapt that raw material wholly to the requirements of expressivity and subjective shading. That would have been impossible with rigid twelve-tone organization, with Webern-like preponderance of serial processes, or indeed with the attempt to derive forms and correlations out of the row itself. Berg's tolerance as regards the row allows for the greatest conceivable differentiation in all other dimensions. That is probably the essential point of technical divergence between him and the two other Viennese masters in their maturity. To the extent Berg paid any attention to questions of row structure, he was more interested in exploiting its flexibility in accordance with his compositional intentions than in accommodating those intentions to the structure of the row.

The fourth song is again less rigidly constructed, looser, more improvisational, but more as if in recollection of the precision of the third song than of the aphoristic second: a prime example of Berg's extraordinarily dense, chromatically intertwined style with its exploitation of minimal motivic ideas. There is a tendency toward artfully obscured octave or unison passages. That technique was originally borrowed from oriental music; Berg may have become acquainted with it in Schoenberg's "Hanging Gardens," which may in turn have drawn on the *chinoiseries* of *Das Lied von der Erde*. Incredibly subtle the way the fourth song is given closure through the shape of the melodic phrases. In the first part, up to the ritardando of bar 15, the curves generally rise, then they descend, unmistakably so in the

66

concluding vocal line. The effect is a kind of retrograde of the whole – not, to be sure, in literal-motivic fact, but in the overall structure – which is prototypical for subsequent large movements such as the Adagio of the Chamber Concerto. The song's tendency toward self-revocation is already presaged in the first section. While the rising phrase entrances continue, an ostinato sonority beginning in bar 9 persists until the song's turning point, so that from early on nothing more really happens harmonically; progress is suspended. This effect leads to consequences in the second part, whose last flute tones clearly refer to the beginning; the effect is continually varied. In such a work it would have been impossible to halt the harmonic flow without affecting the later course of events. As of bar 22 there is another sustained sonority, or, better yet, a thematic chord [*Leitakkord*] of the kind occasionally employed by Schoenberg during his period of free atonality in order to achieve a synthesis of harmony and formal structure. Taken all together the middle songs could be regarded as a tripartite intermezzo, which proceeds from pure improvisation through utmost rigor to a structure unifying both types of composition by implication.

The passacaglia, which moderates its critique of the traditional idiom, also makes clearer reference to tonality than do the other songs, as if the specifically expressive element, which here predominates over everything else, still demanded recourse to the conceptual vocabulary of tonality. That results in bars, around bar 8, which in their general aspect and tone open a vista toward Alwa's music, the first movement of the *Lulu* Symphony.

Clarinet Pieces

The Four Pieces for Clarinet and Piano, Op. 5, are the first of Berg's published compositions to bear a dedication to Arnold Schoenberg. While the earlier works are indebted to Schoenberg as "school" documents, now, after his energetic breakthrough, a master in grateful independence declares his allegiance to a friend. Loyally he follows him into that advanced realm of the undeviatingly expressionistic *moment musical* established by the Six Little Piano Pieces [Op. 19]; to that realm inhabited by Webern's two quartet cycles, as well as their off-shoots for violin and piano, for cello and piano, and the Orchestral Pieces, Op. 10. Of everything Berg wrote, the Clarinet Pieces are the most Schoenbergian; that is why they strive for the kind of stylistic purity Berg usually tends cautiously to suspend rather than affirm. They are strictly "atonal"; there are none of those tonal references usually incorporated by Berg; a single fragmented sixth chord, an augmented triad, or a whole-tone scale hint at the past, but nothing else.

Nevertheless, Berg's individuality becomes evident precisely through the tension with the recognizable model. Aware that the small form is not suited to him, Berg knowingly outwitted himself in the Clarinet Pieces, remaining true to himself even under the powerful spell of Schoenberg's Op. 19. Staunchly confident he selects the one kind of small form possible for him: he makes the technical principle, which that particular form disallows, the very basis for the form.

To be sure, "the smallest link" is an agent of the work's dynamic. It transforms musical substances into functions; [transforms] everything that is into the continuity of becoming. But the consequence of such transformation leads Berg's music to the old Eleatic paradox, which, to be precise, always deals with the finitely small and only by transference with the infinite − a paradox that is not solved as conclusively in his music as it is in pure logic. At any given moment the music, while imperceptibly altered, seems identical with itself: is it not, therefore, standing still? Is not the work's dynamic, when robbed of all material against which to test its dynamism, transformed into stasis? That same question is posed later, on a larger scale, by *Wozzeck*, where the utmost in kinetic activity ceases for a moment of breathless suspense, where time is suspended in space, earnestly submissive to the parodistic words of the Captain, who is frightened by infinity as the contradiction between unending duration and mere moment − until Wozzeck comes to himself and time intervenes to subdue the enchanted circle of his fear.

The Clarinet Pieces were created out of that sudden transformation of dynamism into stasis, out of stilled time itself. Each of them lasts only an instant, like Schoenberg's Op. 19 or Webern's Op. 11; but this instant, which knows no development and no time, nevertheless unfolds in time; the principle of differentiation being implemented so radically that the time in which it governs − which in absolute terms is longer than in the corresponding Schoenberg or Webern pieces − is, so to speak, contracted and made to seem like an instant, whereas by contrast Webern, as Schoenberg said, compresses a novel into a sigh.

Berg's about-face is only possible because of the universal applicability of the smallest link. In the Sonata, and to a certain extent in the Quartet, the smallest link was still operative between themes and owed its dynamic character essentially to the development of one theme out of another as a "consequence." The paradoxical stasis of the Clarinet Pieces no longer knows a "theme"; they are, to overstate the case, music out of nothing. If Berg liquidates the sonata by extending the developmental process over the entire musical structure, here the "material" itself falls victim to that liquidation tendency; if everything is development then any independently defined material loses its meaning. But musical time can only constitute itself in the resistance of material of independent authority; when it flows on without resistance it lacks points of reference and, divorced from time, comes to rest.

The pieces can be interpreted accordingly. Formally they are entirely unstructured and expand upon the prose concept of the last Mombert song. Even sequences are no longer tolerated; motivic development consists solely of variation. Nonetheless the pieces emerge from the liquidation of the sonata. The four movements of a sonata appear in rudimentary, shriveled form; granted, the tripartite form of each movement is transformed in new and surprising ways. The pieces generate their form by everywhere and immediately creating, shattering, abandoning, reintroducing, and rounding off remnants. The first piece, taking the place of an allegro, begins with a short, light two-bar clarinet melody (Example 14). But already its closing phrase (d) is a remnant, a variation of the opening motive (a) by means of interval expansion; at the same time its rhythm, with the tied eighth note, is the rhythmic remnant of motive (c). The right hand in the piano answers the clarinet melody with a third motive, entering with sixteenths that are new, which are immediately imitated by the clarinet and used as a remnant.

Example 14

That motive's continuation in eighths, however, is once again the rhythmic remnant (c), reduced intervallically to a minor second and thereby establishing a connection with the three sixteenths. Finally, the entrance of the left hand in the piano is a rhythmically varied imitation of motive (b) from the first clarinet bar, which had developed there between motives (a) and (c). Through such manifold relationships the beginning is articulated so as to seem like a development [*Verarbeitung*]. What follows merely brings further partitioning; the molecules of the first two bars become atoms. The obvious stasis manifests itself harmonically; no real progress is made, only shifts; the bass note D initially functions as the center of harmonic encirclement. Its dissolution leads in bar 6 to complete amorphousness; the interval of the second is submerged in a clarinet trill. This trill marks the caesura: the piano resumes articulation with a distant variant of the beginning.

Alban Berg

The seventh and eighth bars could be regarded as development; the tiny motive of a minor second is retained as a remnant and its intervals expand; to that the clarinet adds variants of the principal motive (a), characterized by the idea of the large leap which is idiosyncratic to the instrument. In the ninth bar, at the *molto espressivo*, the piano begins a reprise; the first intervals are literal, the rest varied; the clarinet joins in with a reminiscence of the sixteenth-note motive from the beginning in augmentation. Overt tripartite form is avoided by having the reprise, or rather reminiscence, subtly and seamlessly interwoven with the ebbing "development"; and, after the eruption and diminuendo of the middle section, by having the beginning of the reprise seem very much like a closing section or coda and therefore not like a recapitulation of equal significance. The conclusion is again unstructured and static; without allowing any sort of melodic contour to emerge, it sustains an unvarying chordal complex through three bars.

The second piece, corresponding to an Adagio, is, with its idea of the ostinato major thirds, consciously derived from the second of Schoenberg's Op. 19. However, these thirds are not set in a row, like drops, but kept close together, only very briefly abandoned and expanded as a consequence of the chords first introduced in the second bar (Example 15).

Example 15

The resumption of the major third underpinning, though lacking melodic shape, serves as a reprise. Those chords in bar 2 are exemplary for Berg's harmonic language because of the distinctive nature of their *espressivo*. Schoenberg mastered the new chordal vocabulary through his expressive urge, leaving him free to dispose over it as musical substance and to convey subjectivity not so much in harmonic detail as in the integrated whole. Berg clings to the expressive character of harmony. But for him that character is not the pure sound of the internal soul, as it is for Webern. Rather, it is at all times dualistic, or if you will, historical: it contains something

70

Clarinet Pieces

external, something fundamentally alien to the self, and remains taut, dissonance in music that long since seems to have sacrificed consonance as well as dissonance. It is an *espressivo* not of remembrance but of expectation, not of immersion but of threat: in short, Berg's dramatic quality is present in microcosm in the cells of his harmony. It is just such tensely ambiguous sonorities as these that later usher in Marie's murder: the whole piece seems like a first vision of the ostinato pedal scene in *Wozzeck*.

A miniature scherzo, rather like the fourth Schoenberg piece, is the third in Berg's cycle; it is, like all scherzos, more accessible. The scherzo portion is clearly segmented; a supple antecedent phrase, closing with two chords, a rustling consequent phrase, which renders the antecedent phrase immaterial: statically, by means of sustained chords. The middle movement, a genuine trio, which provides the only strong contrast within these pieces, is, on the other hand, itself impervious and without contrast for four bars, timelessly closed within itself; its formal construction anticipates that of later retrograde devices. The reprise of the scherzo portion is radically shortened and merely hinted at motivically. But tempo and tone definitely give it the feel of a reprise. Out like a light.

The special formal concept for the last, somewhat more extended piece, returns later on in Berg's oeuvre; it could be the basis for the *Lyric Suite*'s Adagio appassionato. It is the application to the rondo form of the principle of integral development. The "theme" is made up of a chord sustained over four bars in unvarying syncopated rhythm, with a chromatic opposing line in the clarinet: so, once again, no theme at all. A melodic motive in the clarinet sets things in "motion" [*"Gang"*]; its triplet closing segment comprises the remnant and is developed in imitation; then, following the procedure of the first piece, the music disintegrates through the diminution of all its elements and comes to a complete stop. Return of the opening chords, like a rondo reprise. "Motion" again, this time implemented as a build-up. A variant of the triplet closing segment, entering on the last quarter of the twelfth bar, is the paradigm; this remains melodically unchanged, but, in accordance with the *Kapuziner* principle, is enriched and diminished by ever more notes, and repeated with increasing vehemence; finally in bar 17 there is a percussive effect that erupts in a way reminiscent of the one at the end of the last Mombert song. Coda: a chord in harmonics in the piano, which can be interpreted as a reprise and final dissolution of the thematic chord; above that a clarinet recitative, a free inversion of the still undeveloped opening of the first clarinet figure in bar 5. The harmonic energy of these pieces, pent up over time, has burst its dams, and with it the form: a soulful voice mourns it in sadness.

Alban Berg

Orchestral Pieces

Manchmal hat man so'nen Charakter,
so'ne Struktur.

Sometimes people have a certain character,
a certain disposition.

Within Alban Berg's oeuvre the Three Orchestral Pieces, Op. 6, completed during the first weeks of the First World War, are truly epochal. That eruptive gesture at the end of the Clarinet Pieces, battering down the dams restraining the paradoxically small form, has no relationship to the Dadaist's hostility toward form.[1] With that gesture Berg is free to breathe again, this time so deeply that he forgets all disciplining moderation and reaches toward chaos, the object of his longings ever since his drowsily reticent songs, ever since the tangled configurations of the Quartet. That is the basis on which the music begins to turn: toward the large form, no longer a form redefined, but form following the dictates of its own singular nature. With vegetative force, almost rank, it expands in all directions; the force concentrated so intensely in the Clarinet Pieces as into a single point is now impelled toward total spatiality, its original urge, but one that can only be fulfilled after the most rigorous schooling in compression.

The progress in relation to the Clarinet Pieces can only be compared to the distance separating the utmost in self-discipline from a perfected style; even the brilliant Quartet and the sovereign Altenberg Songs are surpassed by the assurance with which the skills acquired there are mastered here. Harmonic shifts and chordal stasis, that nineteenth-century gravitational pull still evident in the Quartet and Clarinet Pieces, are avoided; the claim to that inheritance takes place on an incomparably deeper level. The primacy of harmonic logic disappears altogether. Technique conquers dimensions before which Berg had hesitated long and patiently: above all, counterpoint. To be sure, there was no lack of polyphonic passages in the Quartet, any more than there was – particularly in Opp. 4 and 5 – a deficiency of intimate knowledge of the instruments. But both were kept within bounds. Now color and counterpoint become productive: they themselves create the form. The first orchestral piece grows out of a timbral idea; the last, with thundering hammer blows, forges together a sprawling polyphony.

---

1 In a letter (recently published in Czechoslovakia) to Erwin Schulhoff, who was murdered by the National Socialists, Berg strongly criticized the Dadaists, essentially for lagging behind the radicalism of the Schoenberg School.

Orchestral Pieces

The new breadth is therefore primarily vertical and not one of duration. "Präludium" and "Reigen" are kept to a modest scale; the March attains at most the length of a brief symphonic movement. But one can speak of breadth in terms other than that of the spacious layering of voices. There is breadth in the stylistic world of the work. Without sacrificing a single one of Schoenberg's discoveries, Berg's insistent elaboration upon his own particular techniques brings him into profound proximity with music external to Schoenberg's orbit: Mahler and Debussy. With these Orchestral Pieces the Schoenberg School merges directly and without detour with the stylistic trends of its time, better yet, reveals itself to be the objectively determinant stylistic authority which ever since its evolution it had in truth rightly been: not an esoteric sect with a private idiom and conspiratorial sentiments, but rather the progressive executor of musical understanding. It carries to its logical conclusion what was merely latent in the more advanced forces of contemporary composition. Admittedly, the Schoenberg School regards these forces as windowless, like Leibniz's monads, but interacts with them all the same in strict accordance with its own concepts. Berg, so it seems, drew a retrogressive connecting line from Schoenberg's musical language to that which preceded it, thereby securing the accomplishments at the forefront through contact with the past. But the retrogressive line extends, as a consequence of its own development, into the future. Certainly not in the ideological sense of the new classicists, who disseminate a warmed-over past as something newer than the kind of differentiation they themselves cannot achieve; but rather in the binding sense that the differentiated response of the grand formal design, which in the Orchestral Pieces constitutes the resemblance with Debussy and Mahler, grows directly out of Schoenberg's statement of the problem — as postulated, for instance, in *Die glückliche Hand* and *Pierrot*. That explains why Berg's most Mahlerian score became the most complicated one he ever wrote. In wild abandon, with multi-note chords and friction between countless simultaneous voices, he far surpasses in sheer provocation everything of which the moderns had until then been capable. The turning point in Berg's style is at once its moment of greatest shock.

The affinity to Mahler was not foreign to the Schoenberg School. With his dedication of the *Harmonielehre* and his grand eulogy Schoenberg passionately declared his allegiance to the symphonist under the imperative of their shared conception of music as what Bloch called "the world's blasting powder." As if by divination, Schoenberg's understanding cut through the stylistic differences to which the superficial ear clings — that superficial ear which no composer deceives more profoundly than Mahler. Later, the funeral march from Webern's orchestral cycle, Op. 6, recalls

Alban Berg

Mahler, as do the march episodes of the slow [first] movement of Berg's Quartet. But only in Berg's Orchestral Pieces is that solidarity with Mahler mobilized into a revolutionary storm.

The position of these pieces in Berg's stylistic development makes that possible. They mark the continuation of Berg's efforts in the Quartet to master large form. Because of the mere awareness of the liquidation process begun there, these pieces can no more take for granted the unchallenged individual identity of themes or even motives than could the preceding Clarinet Pieces. Granted, their dimensions cannot, as there, be founded upon music [created] out of nothing — but there is no given that pre-determines them. It was no different with the anguish that produced the superficial banality of Mahler's themes. Berg's functionalism enters into the most singular constellation with that banality. Actually, the Orchestral Pieces do have themes, which, if generally not paradigms of variative development, at least have concrete melodic contours. But no longer are these themes set down — if only in the manner of the principal motives of the first Quartet — thereupon to have music created from them. Rather, the formal function of the Orchestral Pieces — and the central difficulty they pose to understanding — is to allow the themes to be created by themselves. They do not present the history of their themes, but, as it were, of their prehistoric birth. Yet the source and substance of these themes is not explained entirely by the relationship to Mahler, but also by Berg's relationship to his own prehistory, the parental world of *Jugendstil* and all that subjective illusion, which is gradually being eradicated from his style, in order, as a subterranean and invisible energy source, to fuel the present appearance. If Freud called the substance of his understanding the "flotsam of the world of appearances" [*Abhub der Erscheinungswelt*], Berg similarly recognizes the illusion of traditional musical household effects as debris which he demolishes out of loyalty. That flotsam is the nothingness that vanishes completely among interrelationships; it is the something upon which the aesthetic illusion, even at its most radically constructive, passion-ately feeds. That becomes apparent at the beginning of the third piece, where four shattered old-fashioned march formulae are stitched together and reconstituted into form by the same force that had disintegrated them. From the perspective of the motivic atoms in those fragments the form is seamless. While the Stravinsky of the *Soldier* and the Satie of the *Cinq grimaces* allowed such fragments to stand, bald and inflexible as a mask, Berg's humanity discovered in them the moving force of their decomposition and translated that into the moving force of composition. Benjamin drew attention to those trays in bourgeois parlors on which stamps are mounted under glass in an irregular tableau; one is familiar with the terror emanating from them; how the stamps, glued painfully into place, seem to be twitching *en masse* for all eternity, divorced from their function and therefore banned as a dreadful allegory of that function. In Berg's pieces that sort of montage, allegory, and terror is intensified to express the very embodiment of the dream. Under the glass plates of form, large as a house, in the wild distorted motley array of orchestral planes, those fragments awaken to a second and catastrophic significance. It is the significance of banality. Banality is commodity as appearance [*Ware als Erscheinung*]. If the young Berg's development, like a recapitulation of romantic development, seems like a flight from banality leading to the atom, to the pure moment, then the realization immanent to form marks a turning point: that in the world of commodities there is no escaping the commodity – each [commodity] only more deeply entangled in that world – that the musical atom, once achieved, indeed, ultimately the single pitch, is revealed to be just as banal as the deceptively uniform surface itself had ever been. Berg obeys this law in two ways: through its shape he unreservedly acknowledges the banality of the smallest particle, and he nullifies that particle in the equilibrium of a second whole. The expression of chaos, of panic threat, lying in the tone of these pieces is the consequence of the inordinate power of that kind of integration of banality. If mediocre humanity disintegrates into banal illusion, then the form that reflects that illusion is magnified to inhuman and terrifying proportions. The hammer blow in the third piece symbolizes that. It was used musically twice before: in Mahler's Sixth Symphony as the demonic triumphal march of banality and in Schoenberg's *Die glückliche Hand*, in that scenic moment when the man asserts his full strength, only to be immediately smothered in the sphere of banality. Those two works define the scene of action of the Orchestral Pieces. With a giant's fear Berg piles them one on top of the other. It is fear that they breed.

There are still other ways of approaching the shape of these pieces. Their goal, after the liquidation of the sonata and without a glance in its direction, is the large form. That is why they define that form by means of "characters." In contrast to his earlier music they bear titles that point to those characters; one is tempted to interpret "Reigen" and the March as wrathful play with the nineteenth-century bourgeois character piece, which is wed to banality with an intimacy as fatal as the dialectic into which that intimacy now disintegrates. In Berg's later works that "character" is further developed by means of dramatic, sacrificed humanity: until finally in *Lulu* the dramatic characters are joined with sublime transparency to the characters of form – sonata and rondo. Those prescribed formal models are not taken up intact in the character. They are quoted; the quoted form reappearing, transformed in expression. Only the quoted physiognomy turns it into character. Such quoted characters circumscribe that broken, allegorical quality of Mahler's symphonic style, which is why they are maligned by all classical aesthetics, however veiled. Inserting characters, however, also marks a crisis in the history of new music. Not without good reason did Berg the teacher invariably demonstrate the nature of musical character with the contrasting yet inherently unambiguous pieces of Schoenberg's *Pierrot* – that *Pierrot*, in which the expressionist of *Die glückliche Hand* and the short piano pieces, with passacaglia and mirror canon, but above all with the "Mondfleck" as an inscrutable manifesto, creates musical construction out of freedom. The Orchestral Pieces are characters of this kind; their definition is that of the unambiguous character in name, and the naming, not only in the title but decisively in the internal texture, catapults them out of the wordless silence of absolute subjectivity. That, too, is what places them in proximity to the stage: the folkloristic ruins of the pieces outline what *Wozzeck* expresses; the "Präludium" finds its place in the final scene of the first act, "Reigen" in the first inn scene; from the drumroll of the opera's very first chord the March haunts, silently, noisily, every page of the opera score.

Given that Berg tests all the dialectical movement of his music against paradigms, not just thematic ones in the sense of Schoenbergian variation technique, but also stylistic ones, as if every new thing he ventured emerged from a total variation of something remembered – given that his formal principle still holds the memory of the past, then the first piece, "Präludium," points clearly, in a technical sense, to *Pierrot* and that character of "Mondfleck." As if an allegory had to be found for the turning itself, there is a tendency toward retrograde formations, which from this point on Berg employs continually in his structures as the paradoxical possibility of the repetition of the unrepeatable. To be sure, the "Präludium" offers only the first hint of this. It takes up directly from the conclusion of the last clarinet piece. If that conclusion, the eruption of an incorporeal reality out of form, was associated with Dadaism, then the beginning of the "Präludium" belongs to the sphere of primitivism, as a strictly musical correlate of verbal-optical Dadaism. Pure noise is the residual value of the subjective musical atom against the extra-musical reality of commodities; the strictest and, admittedly, expressionless form of banality and thus the transformation of pure expression into objectivity. The "Präludium" opens with pure noise and in pure noise it disintegrates, like dust; the music in between is an analogy of how music can be wrested from the mute. The same concept, in romantic guise, applies to a number of Mahler's ideas: for instance in the first movement of the Third Symphony. [The "Präludium"] opens with various percussion instruments lacking specific pitch definition, tamtam, cymbals, small and large drum; each instrument is rhythmically so different from the other that the result is an illusion of accidental, random noise. Two pairs of kettledrums join together, forming, as it were, chords: an intervening stage between noise and pitch, in a kind of color row. The timpani chord is taken up by pizzicato strings: the plucked sound continues to maintain the idea of noise. The highest chord tone, e♭″, is accentuated by the solo flute with a flutter-tongue effect in a grace-note rhythm from the noise beginning. At the point, in the sixth bar, where the underlying quartal harmony is modified for the first time, the bassoon, with its denatured high A♮ [a♮′] in the rhythm of the flute note, is superimposed over the distorted sounds. Again, almost coincidentally, a second and then a third melodic note is added, like a grace-note, to the A♮; in that way, out of the strain of those extreme instrumental registers, a motive is born of noise. Trumpet imitation and full ritardando; then, again, a melody of just a single note in that seemingly irregular characteristic grace-note rhythm, reinforced by the small gong: on top of that a soft six-note chord. In its disposition that chord establishes the idea, so characteristic of Berg's mature orchestral style, of the kind of soloistically differentiated instrumentation capable of transforming the self-righteousness of "material" through fantasy, and yet of Mahlerian clarity (Example 16).

Example 16

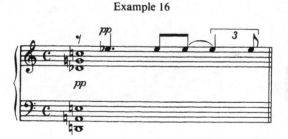

The lowest note is taken by the muted contrabass tuba, the next lowest by the muted cellos, the third lowest by the muted horn, the fourth by the open trumpet, the fifth by the oboe, the sixth by the muted solo viola; the melodic note − e♭″! − is attempted, in accordance with the sonoral concept of employing extreme registers, by the open alto trombone, which rarely ventures into such regions. The orchestrational principle underlying that chord (already discovered in *Erwartung*), is closely related to a harmonic principle: just as the new harmony shuns consonance in the traditional sense as unclear, i.e. as tautological doubling of the single tone and thus "false," so likewise does [new] orchestration tend to shun vertical homogeneity: within such homogeneity single notes would be superfluous and fortuitous and would elude strict constructive determinism. Defined as a technical rule: no two notes of the same timbral family may be direct neighbors in a vertical construction. To be sure, this rule is frustrated by a number of other procedures in Berg's far-ranging orchestrational practice; in Op. 6 beginning with the Mahlerian techniques of doubling and tutti. – Following the trombone passage, a heavy chordal attack: alteration of the introductory quartal chord, added to that, as *Hauptstimme*, a horn and clarinet melisma from the bassoon motive. The long-range effect of the impulse toward brutality is such as to bring forth, between ever more extensive melodic-motivic entrances, passages of idle accompaniment derived timbrally or rhythmically from the noise at the outset. Melodic shape in bar 15: the bassoons repeat unaltered their initial three-note motive (E–G–A♭) and transform it through a twofold axis turn. Assembling such tiny motivic cubes without attempting to create surface thematic coherence defines the resemblance these pieces have to Debussy. It is as if the functionalization of the material had finally severed their functional lines, the motives are mounted like "commas," or, if one prefers, like the stamps, to form planes; no longer the step from motive to motive, but the entire plane is what constitutes the whole. Firmly wedded to that, however, is the technique of linkage [*Technik des Übergehens*]. The violins derive a melodic phrase (Example 17) from the second axis turn of the initial motive, which consequently generates a kind

Example 17

of developmental paradigm. The new motivic segment (17a) is first inverted by flutes and oboes (bar 20), thereby for the first time achieving the motivic shape that dominates the Andante affettuoso of *Wozzeck*; the first violins fuse the conclusion of (17) and the inversion of (17a) (bars 22f.); idle passage and again the initial motive in the second axis turn; then there unfolds an ever more intense, though continually delayed development of the inverted developmental paradigm (17); the declamatory diction of the violin melody, straining beyond itself, translates Mahler's language of a dominant upper voice into Berg's more multifaceted one. Climax (bar 36): multiple thematic combinations, the developmental paradigm in counterpoint with its augmentation (in the trumpets and clarinets), diminution (in the violins) and, for two bars, even double augmentation (2nd and 3rd trombones). Short return, alteration of ritardando and accelerando, dispersing the "undulating" character of the piece into the tiniest of waves. Reprise, beginning with the chord (16), now − symbolizing the caesura − homogeneously orchestrated; the thematic pitch in the flutes and bassoons, though again doubled by the gong. Episodic anticipation of the beginning of the second piece (bars 44f., cf. "Reigen," bars 4f.); variant of the initial motive in the bassoon (bar 46), then augmented in the cellos (bars 47−8). Idea of retrograde: just as the motive in bars 6−8 had arisen out of a single pitch, it now returns, in the solo bass and with complementary trumpet, to a single pitch. The band of noise re-establishes itself, though accompanied right up to the end, even after the dissipation of the pitched music, by a hint of pitch in the kettledrum. Complete collapse into the beginning.

The second piece is entitled "Reigen" and has the character of a stylized waltz. It was the last of the cycle to be composed, in other words after the March finale, and seems to announce the stylistic turning point that the March achieves with blind force; following upon the extreme complexity of the mastered [orchestral] apparatus of the first piece, the second, in awareness of the most effective resources of instrumental music, explores a degree of simplification [in anticipation of] the time when that apparatus will be able to incorporate the stage as commentary; for with Berg, in contrast to the *neudeutsch* composers, the stage provides commentary to the music. He himself regarded "Reigen" as an orchestral study for *Wozzeck*. Relatively long *alla breve* introduction. In addition to its formal structural purpose this introduction serves a second, secret intention: it presents, small as seeds and as if under glass, all the motives that are to come alive under the magic wand of the waltz rhythm: the thematic harmonies [*Leitharmonien*] quoted in the first piece, twice fleetingly anticipated, then complete, in a context whose upper voice soon thereafter becomes thematic (Example 18);

Example 18

the later waltz theme (cf. bar 20), closely related to the waltz theme of the "Präludium," in trumpets and bassoon (Example 19); the direct melodic continuation of that theme in the oboes (Example 20), which is immediately

Alban Berg

Example 19

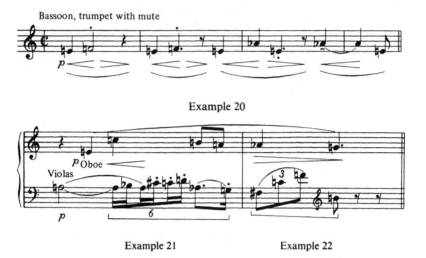

Example 20

Example 21   Example 22

imitated by the horn; added to that an insignificant counterpoint in the violas, which contains two motives (21) and (22) that are later of great importance; and an antecedent-like phrase in the cellos (Example 23). In conclusion a combination of (18) and (21) in the trumpets; then (as of bar 14) a transitional passage: a three-four rhythm is cleverly crystallized out of a violin paradigm by means of overlappings [*Überbindungen*] already introduced at the conclusion of (23). With the introduction of the three-four meter the waltz (23 varied) begins with a simple four-bar phrase in the trumpet and bassoon; the accompanying counterpoint is nothing other than the upper voice of the second bar of (18). The closing phrase immediately abandons symmetry: it had only been in play. The contrasting ideas of the closing phrase are already present in the introduction: bars 24 and 25 (flutes and oboes) comprise the viola motive (21), bar 26 is the by now oft-repeated, related triplet (22), augmented (bars 27f.) by a variant of (23). Beginning in bar 30 the four-bar phrase that entered in bar 26 is presented in a dance-like sequence, albeit shortened and radically varied: the dance gesture relegated, as it were, to the subconscious. The final bar of the

Example 23

sequence is associated, as a varied remnant, with the beginning of the principal theme [*Hauptthema*] and (as of bar 31) related to it as the paradigm of a transitional section; once again extensive variation of the paradigm. Surprisingly, instead of a new dance strophe, bar 42 brings an expansive timbral episode over threefold ostinati with flageolet, tremoli, and glissandi; its motivic substance is the major third [i.e., diminished fourth] of the principal theme and (21). Rushing on, the music regains contour: "*schwungvoll*" ["with verve"], "*fast roh*" ["almost roughly"]. New waltz paradigm in the violins: the opening segment of (23). It is melodically developed with great freedom, like a Mahlerian variant; the continuation of the *Hauptstimme* in the low strings (as of bar 53[54]) recalls the upper voice of (18). The remnant of the long violin melody leads to a development consisting of three sections (bar 55).

This development's first paradigm is initially presented as an extended flute solo; melodically it fuses originally disparate components, among them (20) and the retrograde of (22). Over five bars (as of bar 60) one of its segments is worked out in close detail; then the first violins re-enter (bar 65) with the melodic core of the paradigm. Twofold variation of a remnant, then (bar 69) re-entrance of the waltz, "*derb bewegt*" ["robustly"], with an apparent structural relationship to the entrance in bar 48. But the waltz is immediately drawn into the development, whose second section, employing a remnant from the first, to a large extent comprises (22). The development dissolves in sound, seeps away, and – again surprisingly – breaks off completely in a compositionally irrational manner rather unusual for Berg but similar to the extended development of Schoenberg's Chamber Symphony before its closing section. In Berg, too, a caesura and *General-pause* precede the closing section at this point (bar 82). The last section unfolds over an incomparably rich and complex ostinato derived from the beginning of the development (bar 55[56] flute, bar 56[57] trombone), but adheres to the entity (22) until the section gradually blends into a reprise of the actual waltz beginning. This reprise is elided with the development in that, prepared by a minor second in the horns, it begins (bar 93, horns) while the instruments involved in the last development section are still concluding in full force. By the time the actual waltz reprise emerges openly (bar 95) it has already shriveled to a mere shadow of only five bars. The comfortable triple meter form is remodeled by means of artful recourse to the introduction, whose *alla breve* meter (as of bar 100) is combined with that of the waltz. Berg sets up a counterpoint (as of bar 96[97]) between the original waltz melody and a duple theme in the solo violin, which – using an instrumental-constructive method he continued to cultivate through the *Lyric Suite* up to the Violin Concerto – "increasingly penetrates [the texture]" [*immer mehr durchdringt*]. But it is the inversion of the original upper voice melody (18). That inversion and an on-going recitative give rise to the creation of a combinatorial section that finally (bar 110) leads into the unmistakable reprise of the introduction. The thematic harmonies enter imitatively; then the inversion of their upper voice melody (18) in the rhythm already established in bar 53[54]. Stretto, reduction to nothing but remnants. With these remnants as sustained harmonies, motive (22), which had been the basis of the second and third development sections, now takes on, in the horns, the function of the final cadence.

Only a book such as the one Berg planned on Schoenberg's D minor Quartet could give an adequate idea of the third Orchestral Piece. Words prove an awkward coordinate system for the score that Berg, not without artistic pride, called the most complicated ever written. Any attempt at compressed analysis, already highly questionable in the case of "Reigen," would be both fruitless and confusing for the March. Even in the literature that has meanwhile been published, the March remains terra incognita. Nevertheless, a few general hints may provide useful, if rough, orientation. The technique in "Reigen" − setting up in the introduction, à la Debussy, a series of motives, which as embryos do not take on clear definition until the piece's actual "character" is established − is employed even more recklessly in the March; motivic fragments coalesce into themes without ever acquiring the character of something definite and therefore repeatable. A tripartite A−B−A form is no longer even implicitly suggested; instead there are march strophes created from ever new configurations of the introductory material. It is the critical rethinking of an imposing paradigm: the finale of Mahler's Sixth Symphony. Compressed, it climaxes to a catastrophe so palpable that, like Heym's and Trakl's poetry, it seems to conjure up the impending war. But the idea − starkly abbreviated in Mahler, radically developed in Berg − of shifting the "exposition" into the introduction which precedes the developmental treatment of the main section, is quite obviously bound up with the liquidation of the sonata. That explains why there is no external formal structure: coercive and disorderly, like a cityscape, the movement spreads out before one. The law governing its immense size can only be found in the smallest component. In unceasing variation and just as in the later twelve-tone technique, motives are manipulated as "basic shapes." An example, the decisive first motive, the march fragment in the cellos made up of a [minor] second and [minor] third (Example 24), which permeates the movement in uncounted variants, transpositions, and axis turns; already the second bar trill motive in the clarinets is derived from it. The panic-stricken amalgamation of Schoenberg and Mahler is evident not only in the over-contrapuntalization of the March

Example 24

themes, but also in the very procedures: creating the March out of structural ruins and variative motivic construction.

First section of the introduction (up to bar 15): march rhythm, clarinet trill, march pitch repetition in the English horn, oboe fanfare. The first violin entrance: inversion of the basic motive (24): quasi thematic formulation in the violins and violas as of the eleventh bar. Second introductory section, returning in bar 15 to the amorphous opening material, tension in the percussion. With bar 25, deceptive principal entrance of the March, comparable, for instance, to the passage in Mahler's finale at figure 109; immediately revoked and completely dissipated; important contrasting idea in the solo viola. The March idea is resumed in the same fragmentary guise as the waltz idea in the second piece: initially in a faster "Tempo II" (bar 33). For the third time, mediated by a ritardando, the introductory character prevails, along with a contrasting idea in piano (bar 40). Back to the tone of the second section; but finally the march pitch repetition collapses into the wild horn theme of the main section (bar 53). The trombone motive to which this leads later brings on the catastrophe. A grazioso episode (bars 62f.) is like a solo set against a tutti, but is no longer able to pacify the march character, which immediately reasserts its authority. Homophonic concentration (bar 76), very brief closing phrase [Abgesang] in the violins (bars 77f.); rondo-like return to the tone − by no means the themes − of the introduction; in its structural idea perhaps analogous to figure 120 of Mahler's movement. Rapid crescendo to the second principal section of the March, which expands as in an extremely broad development. The climax is marked by the hammer blow (bar 126); added to that the retrograde of the "basic shape" (24) in the violins. The initial effect of the blow is to atomize [the texture]; however, the March is recovered, the section transformed into a return. Third decisive March entrance (bar 136); functioning as reprise due to the return of the tempo but already severely curtailed. The coda (bar 149, "Tempo III") belongs to Berg's most daring conceptions. The fanfare from the opening breaks through, accompanied by chorale-like half-notes in the winds: anxiety of tellurian proportions. Diminuendo, interrupted once (bar 160). Ritardando, dissolving as an epilogue, again the contrasting motive in the alto trombone. Then, subito

Tempo III, the trombone motive resounds. Very brief crescendo in the brass alone: great and contra E as full stop on the weak beat. In the last sonority the final blow of the hammer.

Toward a characterization of *Wozzeck*

In the case of *Wozzeck*, where the niveau of the musical work equals that of the literary work upon which it is based, it is well to consider the relationship between the two creations. Given a literary work of this kind music could easily seem superfluous, mere duplication of the drama's own underlying substance, of that which makes it a poetic work. In order to understand the relationship between Berg's meticulously crafted opera and Büchner's intentionally sketch-like fragments, to grasp what brought the two together in terms of aesthetic economy, it may be well to remember that one hundred years lie between the drama and the composition. What Berg composed is simply what matured in Büchner during the intervening decades of obscurity. At the same time, the music capturing that aspect has a subtly polemical quality. It says: "What you have forgotten, what you never even experienced, is as foreign, as true, as human as I myself am, and in presenting it to you I am praising that other." *Wozzeck* the opera is intent upon an historical revision in which history is simultaneously relived; the music's modernity accentuates the modernity of the libretto, precisely because the latter is old and had been denied its own time. Just as Büchner obtained justice for the tortured, confused Wozzeck, who, in his human, dehumanized state, objectively represents all soldiers, so it is the intention of the composition to seek justice for the drama. The passionate care with which, as it were, every last comma of its texture is respected illuminates how closed is the openness, how complete the incomplete in Büchner. That is the function of the music, not psychological underpinning, not atmosphere or impression, though elements thereof are never disdained when needed to bring to light those aspects of the work that had been buried. Hofmannsthal once said of the text of *Rosenkavalier* that that comedy for music was meant for music because it was not about what is *in* people but what lies *between* them. That — a kind of interlinear version of its text — is even more true of Berg's opera than of Strauss's. The music does not just set out to describe the characters' feelings, but tries on its own to make up for what a hundred years have done to the Büchner scenes, the transformation of a realistic draft into one that crackles with hidden meanings, in which everything held back in words insures a gain in content. To make manifest this gain in content, this unspoken component — that is the function of music in *Wozzeck*.

Toward a characterization of *Wozzeck*

The music treats the fragment with indescribable gentleness, softening and smoothing the jagged edges, and seeking to comfort the drama over its own despair. Its style is that of seamless correspondence. And it, too, carries the art of transition much further than Wagner ever conceived possible, carries it to the point of pervasive mediation. It does not shrink from extremes, Büchner's tragedy completely absorbs the profound melancholy of the music's south German/Austrian tone, but with such coherence and immanence of form as to give scenic embodiment to expression and pain, serving thereby, purely out of itself, as something like a posthumous court of appeals. The joined and interlaced quality of this music, its seamlessness, is decisive. Should the performance falter just once, should the texture rupture even for a moment, the acoustic whole would topple into chaos. What then arises is, to be sure, an aspect of the thing itself, that dumbstruck *espressivo* requiring the greatest possible constructive and sonoral discipline to prevent the whole from plunging into diffuseness. In general, Berg's music operates in the tension between the importunateness of the unconscious and an almost concretely visual architectonic sense for self-contained planes. He himself said of *Wozzeck* that it was an opera in piano with occasional outburts. Only now that the printed score is widely available is it possible to gauge how true that is.

Long passages, starting straight off with the Suite with which the first act begins, are really conceived soloistically, like chamber music; great complexities are only occasional, and *tutti* are reserved entirely for the few dramatic turning points. Such sonoral economy fosters extremely dense texture because of the absolute clarity and unambiguousness of each musical event. Without being paradoxical one can assert that this difficult creation, which still requires numerous rehearsals, is simple: because there is not one note, not a single instrumental line that is not absolutely requisite for the realization of the musical meaning – and coherence. Truly practical instrumentation gives the lie to all who babble about post-Tristanesque late Romanticism in order to relegate to the past a composition which even today they cannot understand.

The lesson to be learned from *Wozzeck* is first and foremost the meaning of integrated instrumentation [*Ausinstrumentieren*]. The prevailing ideas about orchestration in particular are still such that a painter, for instance, for whom color is a self-evident unifying factor in his work, can only shake his head. On the one hand, the awful phrase "brilliant orchestration" – a musical horse-trading ploy of saddling a score with as colorful and gaudy a garb as possible in order to hide its paucity – has once again come into vogue, as if the most important exponents of new music had not discredited such clever tricks once and for all. On the other hand, those who do not care for such false riches take great pains to cultivate an asceticism that would love nothing more than to ban the joy of all color from music and thus retreat from one of the most significant compositional sectors, conquest of the timbral dimension. The score of *Wozzeck* provides a corrective to both standpoints. The orchestra makes the music real in the Cézannesque sense of *réaliser*. The entire compositional structure, from large-scale divisions to the tiniest capillaries of motivic development, becomes clear through color values. Conversely, no color is used that does not have a precise function in the delineation of musical continuity. The formal disposition coincides completely with the orchestral; concertino-like ensemble combinations and *tutti* effects are carefully balanced. The art of sonoral putty, the subtle flow from one color into another, these are unparalleled. The atmosphere of this orchestra, however, which loses itself in self-forgetfulness in the recesses behind Büchner's words, is no mere mood painting. It is atmosphere derived from the power of nuance, which is synonymous with the power of integrated instrumentation, the translation of even the subtlest compositional impulse into its sensuous equivalent.

Perhaps the score's simplicity can best be elucidated by a comparison with Strauss. In *Heldenleben*, in *Salome*, much more actually happens on paper than one hears in the orchestra; most of what is written remains ornamental or filler material. In Berg, precisely because the orchestra is completely subordinated to musical construction, everything looks almost geometrically clear, as on an architectural drawing, and the full richness of the composition becomes apparent only during performance. There is nothing superfluous in the score, it does not make a fuss, and the most differentiated sounds − like the famous pond impressions in Wozzeck's death scene − occasionally turn out to be as simple as Columbus's egg. What is left out proves to have no less creative power than that which is written: the only economy providing the obligations of form [*Verbindlichkeit der Form*] to Berg's over-flowing musical substance. Some scenes that look terribly complicated in the piano reduction − the fantasy and triple figure of Act II/2, for instance − acquire a plasticity and transparency in the full score that have yet to be matched by theatrical practice, and which Boulez was the first to realize.

The integration of the texture, which despite dramatic expressivity avoids crass and primitive contrasts, is the result of construction. *Wozzeck* was the first stage work of any length to speak the language of free atonality. Absence of tonality made it all the more imperative to develop other means that could effectively establish coherence. Those means are the traditional thematic-motivic techniques of Viennese classicism applied to their full extent and as never before to the stage. It is the task of the orchestral setting, this time of Mahlerian clarity, to delineate the thematic-motivic ideas. It would be misleading to confuse this construction with the oft-cited forms of absolute music employed in *Wozzeck*. Granted, those forms guarantee organization over large temporal spans, but they need not and should not be perceived as such, rather, they are very nearly invisible, somewhat like, later, the rows in a good twelve-tone composition. Incidentally, formal coherence is reinforced by a series of pliant leitmotives of thoroughly Wagnerian, music-dramatic character; the triple fugue in the street scene of Act II, for instance, combines three of the most important of these motives, that of the Captain, that of the Doctor, and the groping triplets of Wozzeck's helplessness. Far more significant, however, is the inner construction of the music, its fabric [*Gewebe*]. At the time *Wozzeck* was composed, countless composers, above all Stravinsky and Hindemith, were searching for a new autonomy for operatic music. They wanted to free music from its dependence upon the poetic word. In *Wozzeck*, too, music makes new claims for sovereignty within opera. But Berg's method is directly contrary to that of the neoclassicists: utter submersion in the text. The composition of *Wozzeck* outlines an exceedingly rich, multi-faceted curve of the inner plot: expressionistic in that it takes place entirely in an inner realm of the soul. It registers every dramatic impulse to the point of self-forgetfulness. For that very reason it is as articulated, explicated, and variationally developed as only great music is, as are the instrumental movements of Brahms or Schoenberg. It gains its autonomy from its own inexhaustible, self-renewing development, while those opera scores that divorce themselves from the scenic action and go their own unrestrained way threaten for that very reason to become monotonous and boring. Perhaps it is the ultimate paradox of the *Wozzeck* score that it achieves musical autonomy not by opposing the word but by obediently following it as its deliverer. *Wozzeck* fulfills Wagner's demand that the orchestra follow the drama's every last ramification and thus become a symphony, and in so doing finally eliminates the illusion of formlessness in music drama. The second act is quite literally a symphony, with all the tension and all the closure of that form, and at the same time at every moment so completely an opera that the unaware listener would never even think of a symphony.

It is not superfluous, particularly today, to point out that *Wozzeck* is an opera and calls itself such. Present-day theater music for opera houses increasingly tends toward film score-like accompaniment, toward radio background noise, toward mere incidental music. In *Wozzeck*, on the other hand, the music, in completely absorbing the text, becomes central and should be the sole focus of attention both for the performance and in listening. With the surest of instincts Berg the avant-gardist prescribes a "realistic" staging, no doubt in order not to detract attention from the music as the most essential element. The music is thematic; in every scene presenting supple motives or themes, transforming them and giving them their own destiny. This music must be thematically performed, too, above all in order that the musical characters become explicitly identifiable and are thrown into relief. It is necessary to follow these themes and what happens to them, whether it be those in the jewelry scene of the second act which, sonata-like, derive from the tiniest motives, or those of the scherzo, the big tavern scene, or the modifications of the variation theme of Marie's Bible scene, with its daring juxtaposition of mythic tonality and convulsive atonality. Despite the timbral fantasy, despite such striking orchestral effects as the B which after Marie's death crescendos to the point of laceration, or the rippling water when Wozzeck drowns – sound is always secondary, the result of strictly musical-thematic events and derived only from them.

If one concentrates on these musical-thematic events as one does on the melodies in a traditional opera, everything else automatically becomes clear, above all Berg's tone: the glassy, hypnotic anxiety of the scene in the field, the march at once muted and crass behind the scene, the lullaby, echo of stifled, resurgent nature; the unspeakably melancholy *Ländler* in the big tavern scene, Wozzeck's abysmal question about time, the uneasy sleep in the barracks. Vulgar popular music, the shabby, tarnished joy of servant girls and soldiers is heard in all its concrete foreignness and becomes music, but not with Stravinskian derision, rather, confined to an expressive realm, that of boundless pity. At the same time the compositional means derived from dramatic fantasy are already so highly developed that they anticipate many things thirty years in the future: for instance, the inclusion of rhythm into the thematic variational technique, which was then rediscovered in serial music: the rapid, coarse piano polka in the opening bars of the second tavern scene is the rhythmic paradigm of everything that then rushes past in the course of the scene. The creation is so complete that nothing is required of the listener beyond a taut readiness to receive what is given with such prodigality. No one should shrink from a love that unreservedly searches out humanity where it is neediest.

Epilogomena to the Chamber Concerto

The Chamber Concerto for Piano, Violin and Thirteen Winds (1925), the first of Berg's compositions without opus number, marks another major turning point in his oeuvre. He would not have been master of the smallest link if the new life beginning with that work were easily identifiable; yet it is unquestionably the archetype of everything he wrote thereafter. The trend toward greater breadth, toward expansiveness, is a development diametrically opposed to the dramatic concentration of *Wozzeck*; for once in the case of this arch-dramatist one can speak of epic music. The younger Berg completely lacks any element of playfulness in disposition or tone; earlier he would probably have disdained terminology like "scherzoso" for the variation theme. Up to this point agility on a large scale was foreign to his quasi static technique; nonetheless this technique *is* preserved in countless other aspects. According to Berg it was Schoenberg who originally suggested that he write a concerto. Whether biographically there was also an element of fear that he succumb to mannerism and become stereotyped by the *Wozzeck* style must remain an open question; it is probable, however, that Berg unconsciously sensed a music-historical trend, as was the case for Schoenberg after *Pierrot*. Both men may have felt the same: that it was impossible to adhere to the expressionistic point of view, the pure expression of the subject in isolation. The thorny problem is how to get beyond that point without illegitimately borrowing from the language of musical form, which that very subjectivity submitted to irrevocable critique. In *Wozzeck* alienation [*Entäußerung*] had to a certain extent been prepared by the operatic form, by the *musica ficta* of dramatic roles; on the other hand, the character of the central dramatic figure, that of the paranoid, literally estranged anti-hero, encouraged the expressionistic gesture within the operatic form, to which it is normally antithetical. In purely instrumental music, which dispenses with such supports, the task becomes more acute. In selecting the concerto form, which Schoenberg himself was to take up twice in later years, Berg attempts a solution with an "As If" like his teacher's *Pierrot* and Serenade. Hence the playfulness. At the same time, older and newer layers are often superimposed in this concerto by the cautiously groping composer, forming complex configurations. That may help account for the extraordinary difficulties the Chamber Concerto has presented both to performers and listeners. Nowhere is that phrase about a transitional work more concretely applicable than in the Chamber Concerto; not until ten years later did Berg retrospectively and with sovereign mastery distill the essence of this work in the Violin Concerto.

The relationship to *Pierrot*, despite the difference between that work's compressed, shriveled themes and the long spun-out ones of the Concerto, extends all the way to the motivic cells. One could consider the interlude following "Enthauptung" in the second section of *Pierrot* (Example 25) as a paradigm for the characters of the Concerto, with whose principal theme it shares the 6/4 meter. To be sure, Berg's much later piece,

Alban Berg

Example 25

From Arnold Schoenberg, op. 21, no. 13

Example 25 contd.

conceived after the First World War, no longer exhibits the idiosyncratically fragmented character of Schoenberg's melodramas: it is freer, more "concertant" music making. The tendency toward a kind of recourse to previously proscribed structural tectonics, to which Schoenberg first resorts in the Wind Quintet, is also at work in the approximately contemporaneous Chamber Concerto. This work once again indulges in themes of the precritical kind and seems, in fact, to be generally something of a reprise of the older idiom in terms of thorough manipulation of material; herein, too, a connection to *Pierrot*. And yet the Concerto is not simply a concerto: actually none at all for the two solo instruments. They are treated with striking circumspection, as if Berg feared recklessly exploiting their potential. Steuermann once complained half in jest that for all its length, in the entire piece the piano, with one exception (the solo in the first variation of the Scherzoso), has no real opportunity to let loose; at best, the big cadenza gives the soloists their chance. Particularly in the Rondo the piano does not always function in a Brahmsian manner, as is usual for the Schoenberg School – i.e., as an instrument for two hands in their chordal positions – but rather for long stretches as an instrument for independent voices. To be sure, there are, by contrast, highly idiomatic keyboard passages, but, surprisingly, these are not a prominent feature in the overall sound. There is, as Berg tended to say in such situations, simply too much music for that.[1] By contrast the most extreme demands are made upon the accompanying wind ensemble. In the rapid tempos the brass in particular are led to the very limits of what is playable. Berg did leave one hint in the now famous dedicatory letter to Schoenberg: a concerto is "precisely the art form in which not only the soloists [...] are given an opportunity to display their virtuosity and brilliance, but for once the author, too." According to that, it is a concerto for a composer, not for concertizing soloists. Under the primacy of the compositional ego the viewpoint of an expressionistic hermit asserts itself. That is probably what motivated Berg to the paradox of having the concertizing protagonists step back, as it were; in any event of rarely giving them the opportunity, to quote Berg again, "to go into action as soloists" in the traditional sense. He wanted to be as complicated as he was, to his heart's content, unimpressed by the aesthetic carnival wisdom after the First War that demanded *clarté* and simplicity in art – though in truth this was only to save the regressing audience from having to work too hard. The concerto form was suited to this propensity of Berg's insofar as it allowed him, too, to frolic and cut all manner of capers. At the same time, however, the insatiability of his compositional process and his joy in combining had to

---

1 Berg hid several droll details in the instrumental parts, for instance the violin *pizzicati* in bars 111 and 112, whereas the solo violin remains silent during the rest of the first movement, or the twelve extremely soft bell-like contra C # notes in the piano at the fulcrum of the slow movement, in which the piano is otherwise entirely tacit; this passage may have been inspired by Strauss's [*Sinfonia*] *Domestica*. Unquestionably these passages contradict traditional ideas of compositorial good etiquette. Etiquette requires that the composer respect the rules established by himself – the violin tacet in the first movement, that of the piano in the second, both instruments joining together only in the Cadenza and Rondo. With as much discretion as pleasure in forbidden fruit, Berg, no doubt intentionally, violated this etiquette and thereby also blurred established boundaries. Being a friend of tangled snarls [*Gewusel*] he balked at the orderly schemata A + B = C, which he himself layed out graphically. The inclusion of quarter tones as chromatic intensification in the Adagio (bars 280 and 441) and in the corresponding passages of the Rondo is part of the same pattern. Already in *Wozzeck* he had ventured the use of quarter tones. And yet it is not, as with Hába, intended as an expansion of tonal resources, but rather as a heightening of the compositional principle of the infinitesimal. The consequences of chromaticism lead beyond the secure realm of the twelve half tones.

be directed toward achieving a meaningfully organized whole. The Chamber Concerto does not ask how to represent a meaning, but rather how something that is overflowingly rich, immeasurably luxuriant, can become meaningful.

That involves limiting Berg's espoused ideal of "commitment" [*Verbindlichkeit*]. In a conversation Kolisch once actually characterized aspects of Berg's noncommittal manner as central to the difference between him and Schoenberg. By that he meant both the nature of their themes – it is seldom that Berg's themes are reduced to their most extreme, precise form, as are Schoenberg's – as well as the sometimes nonchalant use of formal means that normally do not permit nonchalance: for instance, an approximate, not literal contrapuntal layering of complexes. An example is the extraordinarily beautifully conceived closing phrase of the variation theme (Meno allegro, bars 25ff.), in the third bar of which Schoenberg would surely have refrained from repeating the eighth and [dotted] quarter-note motive and gone straight on to the eighth-note figure; but it is precisely that hesitation in the motivic process, that gesture of allowing oneself time, which adds to the expressivity of the passage and thus to its beauty (Example 26).

Dr. Schön's principal theme in *Lulu*, too, contains in its second bar what seems at first glance a superfluous and nonetheless – or perhaps for that very reason – characteristic tone. As much as anything else it may have

Example 26

been phenomena such as these that initially turned the post-Second War generation, who were more interested in integral composition, against Berg. Today, judged from a higher critical standpoint,[2] it is unclear whether those aspects of Berg which with others form a syndrome are really flaws. If it is true that in Berg no musical shape wants to be absolutely itself, that all would prefer to be liquidated, then the concept of thematic terseness loses at least something of its authority. Berg's dynamic nihilism does not spare norms from which, as the precise and conscientious artist he was, he did not wish to abstain. While he came increasingly to reinforce the structural component, already implicitly in *Wozzeck* and then explicitly in the Chamber Concerto, precisely that component's rigid, heteronomic aspect must have disturbed him; initially he was not enthusiastic about the twelve-tone method. Being a musician of Austrian *désinvolture* he approached construction in deadly earnest, but not too earnestly; he groped for a way to rectify it, to mitigate its rigidity with humanity. His primarily aesthetic point of view resisted chaste correctness without fear of the contradictions that involves, also, to be sure, without his or anyone else being able to mediate the antinomy between commitment and noncommitment. Thirty years later young composers had to deal with something analogous when, with hand and ear, they reworked structures that were intended to be produced solely out of the resources themselves: the process was similar in the case of some aleatoric texts in literature. Probably one can do justice to all of these perspectives only by seeing them in relationship to Berg's tone, to his manner of expression that flinches from obstinacy and negates self-assertion. Given tireless self-criticism – and ultimately in the name of that self-criticism – his music does not care to be all that precise and refractory. The second filtering, a refined laxity, is the ferment of its character. His artistic nature was stronger than all his technical training. That may have encouraged his unhesitating inclination toward temporal expansion, as well as toward concertant-like music-making [*Konzertantes*].

The reason the Chamber Concerto has been rather neglected in the secondary literature may have its roots in that letter to Schoenberg, which has been taken, so to speak, as an authentic analysis. It is not; rather, though discussing some intricate details, [it provides] the framework for an authentic analysis or, if one prefers, the work's outline, which the composition itself then fleshes out. The concrete impediments to understanding the work are not overcome by that letter. The measure of those impediments is aurally documented by the recordings in which most things may well be vertically correct, but which, instead of making sense of the successive musical events,

2 Cf. Theodor W. Adorno, *Klangfiguren* (Frankfurt: Suhrkamp Verlag, 1959), 279.

Epilogomena to the Chamber Concerto

serve up mere nonsense [*Galimathias*];[3] anyone interested in fathoming the Chamber Concerto must study the score and avoid the recordings. Moreover, the oft-made assertion about the work's chamber music-like transparency refers solely to the nature of the ensemble and in no way to the compositional texture. This texture is extraordinarily complicated and difficult to penetrate aurally, particularly in the Rondo, which is based on the idea of presenting the Variations and Adagio simultaneously, in a way the composer of *Ariadne* failed to do with opera seria and opera buffa. In Tristanesque fashion, the melodic line undergoes extensive partitioning. The task of joining what has been fragmented is very nearly prohibitive for the conductor.

The beginning of the theme consists of a melody in the English horn, expanding by the *Kapuziner* process and accompanied by two clarinets. Already by the end of the third bar this melody continues in the same instrument with a motive beginning on A, which is from the motto and comprises the letters of Schoenberg's name represented in note names. The critical note A chafes in closest registral proximity against a B and G in the two clarinets and thereupon immediately against an A#, that is, a minor second, in the E♭ clarinet. The collision is motivated by the construction: coinciding with the conclusion of the English horn phrase (and in a way that was later frequent in the developed twelve-tone method) the two accompanimental clarinets in anticipation intone the conclusion of the Schoenberg anagram. But with this A, Berg abruptly abandons the clearly established tonal realm of the first three bars, to which the ear had become attuned; that exacerbates the irritation. The difficulty now coincides precisely with the collision of Berg's new compositional technique and the older one, which still reigns in the first three bars: for throughout the piece the anagram of Schoenberg's name is, as Redlich has pointed out, used more as a row than as a theme. The work's critical passages are generally those whose compositional principles collide with one another in just this fashion.

In the next bar, the English horn's D, concluding the phrase, is assumed by the trumpet. Orchestrationally that transfer is to take place inconspicuously, nothing more than a shift of color on a note that remains the same. Just rendering clearly and without confusion the line from A to D and then effecting the discrete shift of color on the D is a task beyond the scope of the time normally available for rehearsal; in order to make adequate performances of the work possible, prodigally long rehearsals would be no more than economical. The passage cited is actually comparatively harmless, although it causes mischief, placed as it is at the

3 An exception, according to highly competent sources, is the recording by Harold Byrns, which unfortunately was not available.

95

beginning, where it is imperative to delineate the theme clearly; in the Rondo the difficulty of this example is surpassed many times over. Berg could have made the matter easier on himself if from the beginning he had doubled the English horn A in the trumpet. Since he weighed every orchestrational detail with utmost care, since, moreover, he believed that each compositional event could be orchestrated in a variety of ways, one can assume that he rejected that possibility in order better to emphasize the phrase's climax on the D with the trumpet. Caught in a conflict between motivic structure and clarity he sided with the former and, being a pioneer of a new compositional method, accepted moments of apparent clumsiness. It was a simple act of integrity, not the defeat of a great conductor, when Webern broke off rehearsals of the Chamber Concerto. Incidentally, that was quite in keeping with customary practice in the Schoenberg circle, where it was preferable to sabotage performances of one's own works rather than allow the kind of interpretation that neither understands what is being presented, nor even notices its own lack of understanding and as a result flounders musically; in such instances new music actually does sound the way its enemies maliciously wish and imagine it to sound. Despite the ability honed in *Wozzeck* of achieving the most differentiated effects with relatively simple means, Berg the Mahlerian did not always strive for the so-called safe, secure orchestration where nothing can go wrong; only in his last works did he pay attention to that. With anything less than music-making equal to the task, there is in the orchestration of the Chamber Concerto the risk that the line break. That in turn is in keeping with the fact that in Berg's entire oeuvre the harmonic dimension, which is coordinated with color, remains independent, whereas for Schoenberg, who is much more linear, harmony, as he formulated it, "is not at this time a subject for discussion." Clearly this does not exactly facilitate the aural realization of melody and counterpoint, which of course dominate in this work for winds. With such recklessness Berg even in his maturity demonstrated how little his mastery was disposed toward compromise.

At least in one respect the Chamber Concerto's difficulties are the complete opposite of what the listener of new music commonly expects. Like the score itself, the sound and structure of the work give no hint of being disjunct; the Concerto is the polar opposite of something pointillistic. The work does not heed Schoenberg's joking maxim that he who writes chamber music must keep in mind the need for turning pages, in other words must provide for rests; surely in all of new music this is one of the works with the fewest rests. When there *is* a *Generalpause*, as in bar 630 preceding the Rondo development, it marks one of the most important caesuras. And yet in the Chamber Concerto, as incidentally in some other works of Berg, this continuity – which might be expected to facilitate listening in that it carries the ear along and frees it from the necessity of forging connections – has precisely the opposite effect. There are few aural signposts for orientation. The burden of articulation is placed, as it were, upon the listener; it requires concentrated, differentiated perception to distinguish events and follow the formal process amidst the interweaving and overlapping. As in Viennese classicism the simultaneously sounding voices, though each contrapuntal line is melodically complete, are not equal but have varying degrees of importance, that of *Hauptstimme, Nebenstimme*, and accompaniment. The art of understanding consists above all in following the *Hauptstimme* along its often tortuous path; if one is successful in that then the *Nebenstimme* and accompanimental voices, which are of course invariably functions of the *Hauptstimme* and composed in complement to it, automatically become apparent. If, however, as is true in most performances, the integrity of the voices in their relationship to one another is not made crystal clear, the listener is lost.

Further, the demands of thematic combinatoriality, which serve the purpose of condensing the relationships between simultaneous voices, are entirely new (Example 27):

Example 27

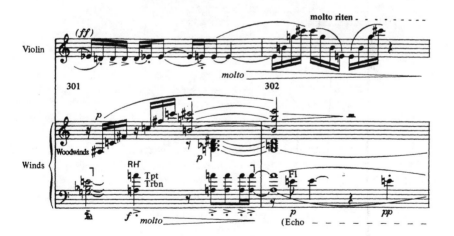

97

Alban Berg

Example 27 contd.

The same theme appears simultaneously in three different note values: trumpet and trombone play it in quarter notes, horns and clarinets in eighths, bass clarinet and bassoon in sixteenths. In addition, the violin (bars 304 to 305) plays the thematic principal rhythm, which is generated in the Adagio according to the principle first tested in *Wozzeck* and later in *Lulu* developed on a grand scale to *monoritmica*. Of course it cannot be expected that anyone but an expert hear all these relationships immediately. The arts employed are there to shape the loose harmonic context contrapuntally so as to make it aurally compelling. The idea of a thematic rhythm was similarly exploited in Schoenberg's Wind Quintet, especially in the Rondo, probably without either being aware of the other's work. Transferring the intervallic dimension into the precompositional material of the row limits the thematic generating force of the intervals. In that way rhythm automatically gains in thematic relevance.

The nature of the entire work is established by the variation theme, the first thirty bars. It is very extended, very different from the expectations one normally has for such a theme. It is unusual not only in length but also in character. Nothing about it, even in the remotest sense, resembles song-like closure. Rather it develops out of itself, dynamically, intricately organized, with a vivacious middle section reaching a climax and then quickly fading away, and an unmistakable, almost coda-like concluding section. According to the internal structure, the opening and middle sections are by no means antithetical, but bound together by a transitional scherzando section (as of bar 8). The inherently dynamic nature of the theme influences the variational process. Berg does not vary the theme as if it were a given, instead he re-thinks the theme's own gestation. Granted, after the first variation, which is, as it were, a written-out repeat of the theme's non-existent repeat signs, there are major transformations making use of the ideas of inversion, retrograde, and retrograde inversion, whereby Berg intended the three middle variations employing those means to be understood both as variations in their own right and as the development section for the movement as a whole. The last variation is therefore meant as a reprise, although with extreme modifications and with immensely complicated canonic formations. While the three middle variations coalesce into a single unit, they are differentiated from one another and contrasting in character: the second is based on a waltz rhythm and remains *Ländler*-like, the third, *kräftig bewegt* [powerfully agitated], is often chordal, the fourth, *sehr rasch* [very fast], is the most clearly scherzo-like, in $6/8$ meter. The third introduces for the first time a proto-type that appears in the later Berg: in the middle piece of *Der Wein*, in the athlete's passages in *Lulu*, also in dramatically important passages of the Violin Concerto: that of pounding chordal catapults [*Akkordschleuder*]. It is probably meant as a counterweight to the principle of the smallest link. From the very beginning (cf. bars 128ff.) the principle of chordal catapults, about which there is something pointedly coincidental, has been linked to a practice that was to become popular twenty years later, the tone cluster, and can, incidentally, be traced back to Debussy: one of the methods by which Berg ingeniously disrupts the realm of pitches by adapting noise.

In his overview Berg characterized the Concerto's middle movement Adagio as being "based on the tripartite song form," apparently because the first half of the movement, proceeding in a forward direction, contains a reprise of the first theme as of bar 331, not an unusual procedure for the mature Berg when articulating expansive and ramified forms. And yet the tripartite idea does not really adequately describe the design of the movement. Specific to it is the extraordinary abundance of themes of generally equal importance. None is merely subsidiary, although they are certainly treated with varying degrees of intensity and at various lengths. While the Adagio, particularly its first theme, opens rather homophonically in comparison with the Rondo, its very thematic abundance, corresponding to the five different principal tempos, threatens to disorient the listener. The disadvantages of a wind ensemble become apparent at a slow tempo; even given the greatest suppleness of compositional treatment and the most loving performance, that ensemble offers more resistance to Berg's intentions than strings would have. Berg's penchant for blending sounds by diminishing one color to pianissimo and leading pianissimo into another, without calling attention to the new entrance, is made more difficult by the fact that not all winds have the same pianissimo or even the same piano, and in fact generally cannot be combined as seamlessly and uninterruptedly as a full orchestra. For instance, if the lowest note of an accompanimental chord is accented by the trombone, the instrument carries so much weight that it almost automatically creates the impression of playing the *Hauptstimme* and would divert attention from the actual melody should that be given to a clarinet in a weaker range. That type of problem permeates the Adagio. At the same time, despite the transitional principle prevailing here, as well, each of the individual themes is clearly profiled. The first, shifted [metrically] three times, is spun out extensively and is chordally accompanied: in one passage two clarinets and the bass clarinet imitate a string tremolo, just as voluminous woodwind chords later imitate the full registers of an organ. The second theme is distinguished from the first, especially in the texture: very thin, independent voices, widely spaced. The third, of central significance for the course of the entire Concerto, is given to the clarinet: one of Berg's most beautiful lyrical inspirations (Example 28). The theme is broadly developed and brought symphonically to a climax (bar 314). After its rapid diminuendo there follows a fourth, sluggish theme (Tempo V, bars 322ff.) and the varied reprise of the first (bars 331ff.).

The disposition of the Concerto as a whole initially precludes a development section since of course the Rondo functions as a development of both the first and second movements. By the same token, any traditional kind of development in the Adagio itself is ruled out by that movement's thematic wealth and by the quasi-developmental character of the third theme. The Adagio also takes part in the liquidation of the sonata form. Simple or

Example 28

varied repetition of the exposition without development, something to which Berg later had recourse in the first movement of the *Lyric Suite*, was not possible because of the considerable length of what according to the formal design would constitute the exposition (bars 241–330). Repeating such an intricate structure would have been out of all proportion to its level of differentiation. This situation: no development, no repetition, and yet the need for formal balance and coherence, automatically invoked, as it were, the expedient of a retrograde of the entire exposition. As in many of Mahler's movements – the Adagio of the Ninth Symphony – the retrograde nature of the form as a whole is meant to effect a closure no longer guaranteed by the formal scheme of music whose very fibre is unsuited to that scheme. Row technique was derived from compositorial macrostructure no less than from microstructure. What prejudice has deemed to be calculated artistry actually has its compelling artistic reason: the need to eschew ossified identity, and to refrain from further and superfluous developing of what has already been developed.

Because the long movement turns back on itself, the second half truly manages to achieve the non-identity of the identical. That this is very much an artistic matter and not an abstract construct, is clear from the way the retrograde passages are fashioned. They reveal something unreal, something derivative in the Chamber Concerto, particularly in the wonderful third theme. For Berg's themes, like Schoenberg's, always manifest a quality of genuine inspiration. They are not – or only rarely – the result of construction. This inspirational quality must perforce be lost in retrograde. That retrograde is of secondary origin. An objective (in the higher sense) compositional process must preserve this secondary quality as an objective aspect of the creation, indeed, must emphasize it and make the retrograde formations recognizable as derivations. The lack of plasticity that sets retrograde formations apart from their original shapes has to be worked out and articulated. Only where the pure row, without primary themes or motives, is the basis for composition, as later in the serial school, only there are the basic shape and its retrograde of fundamentally equal importance. Advantages and disadvantages are in perfect balance. By carefully preserving the retrograde's derivative character, Berg articulates its relationship to the theme, creating several planes on which the partial whole is present, and differentiating between its setting and its functional identity. Later a more consistent technique no longer allowed that. On the other hand, as Berg himself pointed out with regard to the second half of the Adagio, in order to make meaningful the reversal of something already meaningful – something not from the outset conceived for retrograde treatment – the retrograde principle is not employed strictly but rather, in Berg's own words, "partly in free presentation of the thematic material in retrograde, and partly [...] in exact mirror image." To the ears of the twelve-tone and serial purist, the aesthetic sensibility necessitating such operations mars construction through subjective randomness.

Two details of the work deserve special attention. One is the transition of the slow movement to the Cadenza which, wild as it is, is derived note for note from the two preceding movements. Its beginning, with the piano's triple forte following the Adagio, which had died away in quadruple piano in the violin, marks the only abrupt contrast of the Concerto, a contrast made necessary to insure the plasticity of the formal structure. But it is as if Berg's concern for secure mediation had scarcely been able to bear the contrast required. Even here he wanted to reconcile that contrast with the Wagnerian art of transition. He set himself the literally paradoxical challenge of crassly juxtaposing extremes of pianissimo and fortissimo with a surprise effect, creating at the same time a kind of dynamic continuum, like squaring the circle. Playfully and ingeniously he made the impossible possible. Because while the violin and wind ensemble become inaudible at the end of the Adagio, the piano begins just as unnoticeably four bars earlier, as a kind of upbeat, and climaxes to fortissimo with the *attacca* figure on the last eighth of the Adagio, so that its bold appearance is prepared by a gradual crescendo. Yet all of this takes place, as it were, behind

the scenes. The piano, tacet during the second movement, is scarcely noticeable when it first appears in its preparatory bars. It does, to be sure, make a
noise-like rumbling, perceptible in the sub-contra range, but to the ear the
main melodic interest, although steadily diminishing, remains in the piccolo
and violin. That is how the extreme contrast is realized as well as − for the
subcutaneous perception − mitigated, a *tour de force*, rather as if Berg had
wanted to mock himself. Naturally the over-all effect remains subject to the
logical premise of contradiction. The principal gesture remains one of dying
out, the piano crescendo mere background; Berg composes for various
levels of perception, both conscious and unconscious.

And then the conclusion, which, without exaggeration, can be called
unique in new music. Since the end of tonality and the formal genres intimately bound up with it, the most difficult question, just as in drama, has
become how to conclude. The formal design itself no longer guarantees a
definitive end, and cessation based purely on the individual compositional
context almost always carries with it the taint of randomness, as if the piece
had just broken off and could as easily keep going. The extent to which
Berg's imagination was preoccupied with that question is demonstrated in
the *Lyric Suite*, which forsakes a conclusion and divines the shape of the
ending out of that very impossibility. The Chamber Concerto, on the other
hand, strives for and achieves an authentic *fine*. It would hardly do to force
an harmonic cadence, although he includes one of those, too (bar 780). But
as everywhere else, Berg refrains from force: the themes must, as one was
wont to say in the old days of the Schoenberg School, live out their lives and
be liquidated. At the same time there is the need for a convincing conclusion.
With the greatest energy, from the lowest to the highest register, the piano
stacks up a succession of pitches (bar 780) which bear the stamp of something definitive and call forth a decision. Concurrently with this complex,
which is sustained over six 4/4 bars, the violin and winds bring back motives,
among them the Schoenberg anagram (trombone) and the Berg anagram
(trumpet) from the motto. By means of ever longer fermatas the melodic
fragments are separated between bars, becoming shorter and shorter until
they disappear. The conclusion as a whole forms a kind of parallel to the
introduction of the cadenza; the thundering concluding chord in a very
striking voicing remains operative, but the vitality of the motives, of the
lines, dissolves. Yet in order for this to be effective, an interpretation must
establish the conclusion as the logical outcome of the preceding Rondo
development, particularly of its stretto.

Alban Berg

Lyric Suite

Of all of Berg's works the *Lyric Suite for String Quartet*, next to *Wozzeck* and the Violin Concerto, has become the best known. If there is any truth to Kierkegaard's precept that one must be seduced by truth, then the *Lyric Suite* is the test; there is no music imaginable that shapes its resources with more seductive power and yet without once making dishonest stylistic concessions or imposing external constraints for the sake of polish and euphony. Loyalty to appearance [*Schein*] elevates rigor itself to a structural principle; so inexorable is Berg's demand for consistency of appearance [*Erscheinung*], indeed, for the effectiveness of everything which appears [*alles Erscheinende*], that the result is a new compositional criterion as binding as that premised upon absolute material integrity, with which, in the end, it coincides. That is why the *Lyric Suite* leads to the world of *Lulu* and to Berg's late style as a style of second sensuousness. The *Suite*'s success, thanks above all to the unflagging efforts of the Kolisch Quartet, refers back to the very heart of the work; but its greatest and most paradoxical success is in having no reason to be ashamed of that.

On the other hand, the success *is* astonishing. For this example of mature, often playfully superior mastery is a virtuoso work of despair. There is not a single bar that disavows the musician of the two tragedies between which it was conceived. Lacking as it does any illustrative intent it certainly cannot be mistaken for a tone poem in the *neudeutsch* sense. And yet it is a latent opera. In his introduction to the score Erwin Stein called the *Suite* lyrical-dramatic. And in the sense specific to Berg, already noted in connection with the Clarinet Pieces, that is an accurate description. The lyric ego expressing itself, freed of all programmatic reification, is its own dialectic: it has but to sing what it feels and — thanks to its own innate humanity — it becomes a part of the world of which it sings. A painful world: one that remains unattainable for the self, which nonetheless remains longingly bound to it. That Tasso and Antonio, in their lyrical selves, are one and the same, does not preclude the fact that, in their dramatic selves, the latter becomes the undoing of the former. Thus the *Suite*, like [*Torquato*] *Tasso*, closes without being able to close, endlessly open; despairing because the musical protagonist — Wozzeck and Alwa are likewise such protagonists — cannot master the alien world through love; endlessly open because despair only throws them back into the phantasmagoria of their own selves, from which there is no escape.

That world of the lyric hermit, a world that greets him only in parting, is also the world of Mahler's *Das Lied von der Erde*: "Dark is life; dark is death!" The *Suite* is indebted to that work for its hovering, intermediary form, which yet allows the underlying, original form types [*Ursprungstypen*] to become more clearly crystallized than works that purposefully set out to be a song, symphony, or quartet. One long gaze captures the vanishing reality; totally inspired, with no trace of unresolved conflicts and yet real enough to accompany the lyric self along six temporal stages. That is the reason for the fourth movement quotation from Zemlinsky's *Lyric Symphony*, a work that had striven for the same intermediary form. Yet its earliest formulation may have been in Schoenberg's second, vocal, string quartet. There can be no doubt that in the *Lyric Suite*, his second quartet, Berg once again reflected back upon that work; "Take my love, give me your happiness," is its dream, and the Adagio stands in the same relation to the other movements as does the "Litanei" in the Schoenberg work.

Yet the work is not called Second String Quartet but *Lyric Suite for String Quartet*. The stamp of Berg's meticulous sense of form is evident even in the title. As a latent opera, the Suite has the character of an accompaniment, as it were, to a course of events absent from it. But this course of events does not demand the symphonic presence of sonata form as represented in the linear logic of four autonomous voices. Granted, the lyrical reflex of dramatic action is entrusted to the overall sound of the quartet. But that sound approaches that of the orchestra. It is not merely because the wealth of lyrical nuances can only be reflected in a wealth of differentiated instrumental colors. A dramatic-expansive homophony is operative in the *Lyric Suite*, a deep breath after the unrestrained polyphony of the Chamber Concerto Rondo. Often enough the *Suite* allows for no linear articulation and coalesces instead into streams of chords. An ideal accompanist, the quartet virtually carries an orchestra along with it. That is why the *Suite* is just written "for" quartet, ever ready to transform itself into an orchestra, and the fact that Berg ultimately published an arrangement of the middle three movements for string orchestra is indicative of more than the mere caprice of a virtuoso composer: he himself revealed the work's double meaning, in keeping with his uncompromising intent to hide nothing. If the lyrical nature of the *Suite* is best fostered in the quartet, its dramatic nature is best fostered in the string tutti; only here are its contours dissolved as completely and enigmatically as the accompanimental concept of the sound demands; and only here does the paroxysm attain its full catastrophic force.

Contrary to the spirit of sonata form as it is, more a suite of lyric-dramatic moments than the objective articulation of the passage of time, the work, on the basis of its very content and structural sense, demands the liquidation of the sonata, and it completes this task within the continuum of Berg's entire oeuvre. The first movement summarizes the liquidation process once again; the others have nothing more to do with sonata forms.

Alban Berg

But if the *Suite* presupposes the liquidation of the sonata, in particular the achievement of the First Quartet and the Clarinet Pieces, then it is thanks to that achievement that the Suite is given a new freedom with regard to pre-existent forms. The development technique has become total; there is no longer a single note that is not the result of strict motivic development. Meanwhile the more expansive forms require precisely the kind of articulation that had previously resulted from motivic work, which has now been subsumed in the "material" itself. Thus a *new* level of articulation is built upon and governs this material. A second formal sphere submits docilely to the second sensuality. Traditional forms are applied to material already predisposed by motivic development: that is what produces — in the very midst of that obscurity inherent to expression — the assured freedom of effortless virtuosity. There is a rondo and two scherzos; as well as movements that mock formal schemata without, however, losing all connection to them. Moreover, once again there are themes, often expansively spun out, and broad planes of exposition. All of that is reminiscent of the effects of Schoenbergian twelve-tone technique, which permits a similar invocation of traditional forms at the very point at which these forms, handed down directly, are completely subsumed by the material. Indeed, it was in the *Lyric Suite* that Berg first accepted the twelve-tone technique. But it does not reign supreme, rather it is bound up with the resources of free atonality, is, in fact, unnoticeably developed from it. Thus even the palette is preconceived: the outer movements are twelve-tone, the two scherzos set forth their contrasting ideas right to the point of twelve-tone disposition: in the Allegro misterioso the scherzo is strict, the trio free; the opposite is true of the two trios in the Presto delirando. The truly lyrical movements affirm their unrestrained subjectivity by avoiding the twelve-tone technique. However, that technique, even where it is used, is seamlessly bound up with the style of freedom. Berg achieves that through cunning simplification of the technique. He consistently avoids the simultaneous combination of multiple row forms in the interests of a basic homophonic approach; on the other hand, the row is often divided up among a number of mutually complementary voices, which produce the row dynamically. The rows themselves are constructed in such a way as to allow for tonal chords, which are no more absent in the *Lyric Suite* than elsewhere in Berg, and even make the *Tristan* quotation possible. Finally, Berg's functional way of thinking seizes upon the resources of the row itself: it is not retained in a single form, rather, it is constantly modified from one twelve-tone segment to another. The original row underlying the first movement: F−E−C−A−G−D−A♭−D♭−E♭−G♭−B♭−B was one with which Berg was frequently preoccupied; it is, for instance, used in the second setting of the Storm song, "Schließe mir die

106

Augen beide.'' In an analytic outline for the Kolisch Quartet Berg calls it "the twelve-tone row discovered by F. H. Klein, containing all twelve intervals'').[1] This row, with an exchange of the fourth and tenth notes, is introduced in the otherwise "free" second movement (viola, bars 24–28f.) and in that new form is the basis for the twelve-tone passages of the third movement. It appears in a more complicated transformation in the trios of the fifth movement; the finale retains it as a fundamental in the final form: F–E–C–F#–A–C#–G#–D–E♮–G–B♭–B.

The six movements, like their material, are interconnected. The principle of the smallest link has permeated the architecture to such an extent that, in Stein's words, "a theme, idea or passage of one movement always reappears in the next." But the tectonic plan of the whole goes beyond that. The enigmatic compulsion for security of construction with which the mature Berg became obsessed from the time of the Chamber Concerto on – as if in fear that some centrifugal force could explode even the most meticulous structure, he sought to hold construction mesmerized with a multiplicity of simultaneous forms, which themselves sometimes take on the appearance of chaos, like some powerful hallucinatory universe – this mythic compulsion toward the closed security of formal immanence is also operative in the *Lyric Suite*. Whereas the Chamber Concerto had in a rondo presented variations and an adagio in counterpoint, in the *Lyric Suite*, as in a critical passage of the Concerto, Berg's insatiable appetite for paradox unites within the work's over-all outline the minimal step with extremes of contrast. The schema for such a formal paradox is the fan, which at its base is pressed closely together only to flare into extremes. The movements of the *Suite* are arranged in fan-like formation; their unfolding is the dramatic crescendo of the latent opera. The first, introductory movement is entitled Allegretto gioviale. The following Andante amoroso is a contrast more in tone than tempo. The Allegro misterioso and Adagio appassionato follow as middle movements. Catastrophe and epilogue demand extremes of tempo: Presto delirando and Largo desolato.

The first movement is liquified sonata in the extreme. It retains the firm outline of the sonata exposition. Being a twelve-tone piece, it is pure development. From this constellation of factors Berg draws conclusions that had already been prepared in the Piano Sonata, where the development was treated as simplification. Now the development, the dialectical driving force of the sonata form, is absent altogether. The sonata falls victim to the universality of its own constructive principle. The structural experience of Op. 1

---

1 It belongs to the type of "all-interval-row" that Ernst Krenek discusses in greater detail in his book *Über neue Musik* (Vienna, 1937).

illuminates the *Suite* in other ways, too; the transition is fused with the principal section, the thematic characters emerge seamlessly one out of the other, only one, the main theme (Example 29) is shaped with greater plasticity.

Example 29

The reprise (bar 36) is joined directly to the exposition as if, as in the jewelry scene in *Wozzeck*, trying to compose out the repeat signs. One of Berg's last letters explains the meaning of that procedure. "The fact that the first movement is in strict, albeit short first-movement form does not undermine the work's lack of sonata character, since the movement is in no way perceived as a sonata, but more as a light Intrada to what follows." In these dissonantly cheerful 69 introductory bars the sonata is buried alive so as to preserve the structure of the *Suite*.

If the "Präludium" is like a latent opera scene set in the open, then the second movement is an interior domestic scene. It is lyrical throughout, as hopelessly gentle as only Alwa's music later, heightened, to be sure, in its passion, yet gently summoned back into a repressed tenderness. Brief as a poem, the piece is nonetheless intricately organized and contains a wealth of thematic ideas; to understand it one needs above all: to follow the organization aurally. It is a rondo with three themes. The first introduces the gentle, tentative basic character with a bipartite, rounded upper voice melody. Bar 9 seeks to begin a repetition. But it is already developing its material by juxtaposing the principal motives [*Kopfmotive*] of the antecedent and consequent phrases, spinning out the latter with "axis turns." Finally, descending chordal scales bring the texture to a simple close. These scales appear at important points throughout the movement and unify the form. Initially they lead to the second rondo theme. This theme enters somewhat more energetically than the first and, in contrast to that theme's intricacy, is deliberately simple: *Ländler*-like in 3/8 meter (bar 16). It is sequenced unabashedly until the first reprise of the principal theme (bar 41), which, as of bar 36, has been prepared by associating the abbreviated incipit of the second theme with the principal motive of the main theme's consequent phrase. The reprise of the first "manipulation" [*Verarbeitung*] of the principal theme is expanded to a brief developmental rondo-"episode" (as of bar 48). A ritardando mediates the entrance of the third rondo theme

108

(bar 56). Its beginning is marked by a pulsating C in the viola. The theme plays quietly to itself, as if absorbed in some childhood revery; an instant of the kind of music one can never forget. The consequent phrase (bar 65[66]) entirely loses itself in dreams until the pounding re-entry of that C (bar 73); "the way one threatens children," was how Berg once characterized the passage at a rehearsal. Then, as if beginning, the second reprise of the principal theme enters (bar 81). It returns in what follows to a previously insignificant accompanimental motive from the conclusion of the principal theme (Example 30) and forces a development of the tone and rhythmic character of the second theme, though with the inversion of the principal theme's opening motive as a melodic "paradigm" (upbeat and bar 91) that only gradually becomes incorporated into the motivic material of the second theme. The reprise of the second theme is finally reached (bar 101), but is interrupted after only four bars by the third theme ("subito poco meno mosso"). Once again the second (bar 110) and third (bar 113) themes are placed like a new strophe in close juxtaposition, and "senza espressione" the viola shyly announces the first theme in counterpoint (bar 114). But now the music stubbornly insists upon the motives of the second theme; even the languid consequent phrase of the third theme cannot appease it. The second theme remains the *Hauptstimme* in the viola until that revelatory moment in which, high above everything else, including the *Ländler* motive and the threatening, fixated C, from far, far away and emerging only gradually into the foreground, there unfolds the wide arch of a melody in the muted violin (bar 131). Yet this is nothing more than the augmented consequent phrase of the principal theme: the beginning of the last reprise. As the C on the open viola string sinks back into silence, the beginning of the principal theme appears in its original form. Vehement gesture of defiant ecstasy as in the conclusion of the First Quartet; likewise merely the inversion of the beginning of the principal theme. Then the rapidly descending chordal scale prepares the end: the deep C, pizzicato, repeated for the last time, unappeased.

Example 30

The emotional fan unfolds rapidly: the Allegro misterioso is a complete contrast to the second movement, both in tempo and in basic idea. It is not so much the play of intertwined themes as a breathless timbral poem, composed entirely out of stifled, unrecognizably alienated note values, mostly *sul ponticello* or *col legno,* muted throughout. Those who love poetic associations may be reminded of a desperately passionate scene in suppressed whispers, which erupts but once, only to revert again to feverish whispering. The form is that of a scherzo. The actual scherzo portion, constructed from an ingenious segmented twelve-tone row, gives rise to scarcely a single melodic shape; it dashes along in a wild rustle and its course is one of continuous self-dispersal, ever more hasty and impetuous. The Trio estatico brings the eruption: an upper voice melody in wide, stormy intervals (Example 31), soon continued by the chordal scale from the second movement, which discovers its full affective force only here. The repeat of the scherzo once again attests to Berg's determination to secure the form through combinatoriality. Using the "retrograde" of a basic shape is one of the resources of the twelve-tone technique employed in the scherzo. But at the same time its repeat is itself the retrograde of its original form, following the example of the "Präludium" from the Orchestral Pieces and the Chamber Concerto Adagio. The reversal of the sequence of events is quite literal, beginning with the last note and ending with the first; only a middle section is excised. The trick finds its justification in the idea; nothing could capture more drastically the sense of hopeless confinement than the circular closed form.

Example 31

The expressive content of the entire work is concentrated in the fourth movement, Adagio appassionato, which emphatically lays bare what has heretofore been kept silent or merely whispered. Its function is that of a development section and it is arranged as such, tightly compressed and completely homogeneous. Its substance is a single theme (Example 32), created from reorderings of the motives of the ecstatic trio, structurally similar to the variation paradigm of the "Litanei." Already developed during its first appearance, the theme in free four-voice stretto rises

Lyric Suite

Example 32

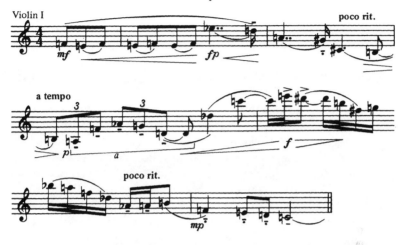

aggressively out of a grinding gesture. Instead of contrasting ideas there are
either quotations of ideas from earlier movements or free "episode"-like
continuations of the principal theme. On the model of the last clarinet piece
the form is articulated through a return of the grinding motive from the
opening, so that the ideas of a developmental paradigm and a rudimentary
rondo are, so to speak, superimposed. A short combination of the triplet
motive (32a) with the main motive climaxes in the first eruption, an overt
quotation from the trio beginning (cf. Example 31). After that, with tension
continuing to build, the three closing bars of the principal theme are developed until, dying away as the first rondo reprise, the grinding motive and
principal theme reappear over surging tonal chords (bar 24). New episode
(bar 27), again created out of the trio melody and motive (32a). This motive
is subtly transformed into the principal theme of the second movement,
followed literally by the motive from that theme's consequent phrase (bar
31). The Zemlinsky quotation leads to the triple forte climax (over a syncopated E♮) in the cello that is reminiscent of the ominous C in the second
movement. The appassionata character is propelled into another eruption
(bar 40, cello), based on an apparently new motive that dominates from this
point on: it is the transposed retrograde of the beginning of the Allegro
misterioso (B−F−A−B♭ = D♯−A−C♯−D). In a recitative-like molto
tranquillo episode (bar 45) the movement reaches its caesura; thereupon
third entry of the grinding motive (bar 51) as rondo reprise. The eruption
and recitative have, however, undermined the dense texture; the grinding
motive is not taken up again by the principal theme. It breaks off with
violent, gesticulating accents. Then (bar 59) the violin, *flautando*, enters

with the "new" motive to begin the coda. In augmentation it reinstates those portions of the principal theme omitted at the last reprise. The movement ends pianissimo, but the sound is not so much dissolved as concentrated, as if with firmly closed lips. The idea behind the closing scene in *Lulu* is no different.

Wildly erratic as the Presto delirando is, it is the simplest piece of the entire *Suite*: scherzo and trio twice in striking alternation, the way Mahler, following Beethoven's example, loved to treat the form. The entire movement is conceived rhythmically-homophonic in a way rare with Berg. Its scherzo section has two main ideas, the first in $3/8$ meter, the second (bar 15) in duplet eighths or whole bars. In bar 36 the cello inaugurates a short concluding figure, which applies the duple accent to the triplet eighth rhythm. The twelve-tone trio ("Tenebroso," bar 51) is based on the idea of "alternating chords," a purely coloristic effect consisting of harmonies entering inaudibly, first *flautando*, later bridge *tremolando*; hence, completely vertical. Turbulence is maintained solely through a very skillful rhythmic disposition of the chordal entrances, which are first compressed, later completely diverge. The first repeat of the scherzo brings its two formerly disjunct main ideas closer together. The return of the trio has somewhat greater contour, the chords join together melodically, and at one point the three eighths from the main section reappear. The close of the trio prepares the main section's second idea, which at its renewed return (bar 321) leads the way. This reprise serves a developmental function. The two main ideas are variously combined and the melodic beginnings of the second trio become thematic. The coda, reaching back to the first concluding idea, stubbornly turns on itself; the duple paradigm interrupts three times and compels the conclusion as catastrophe.

After that the Largo desolato is nothing but an epilogue of sorrow, granted, also its most powerful eruption. The old finale problem becomes a paradoxical formal idea as had the sonata problem in the first movement. If, after Beethoven, no finale was able to close in affirmation, this one simply adopts the principle of infinity as the expression of the finale's negativity. It thereby pays homage to the liquidation of the sonata. It is emancipated from any preconceived formal scheme; Stein calls it "rhapsodic." Yet there are connections to the preceding movements, somewhat as in Schoenberg's "Entrückung." There is strophic articulation, mostly by means of broad declamatory entrances in an accompanimental *Hauptstimme* on the rhythm (33a). Six bars of pizzicato introduction, simultaneously compressed and retarded, then hesitating. Thereupon a short, extremely taut violin melody (Example 33), which recalls in tone, if not in pitches, the Trio estatico. The cello adopts it freely together with the rhythm (33a), then the viola adopts it

Der Wein

Example 33

literally as a theme (upbeat and bar 13). A one-bar paradigm (*col legno*) provides the basis for a contrasting intonation (bars 16 and 17). The strophe rapidly rejuvenates itself and collapses on the contra B of the cello, whose C-string has been tuned down a half-step. Third strophic entrance (bar 22): the section's unity is established by an eighth rhythm treated quasi-imitatively; it closes with the *Tristan* quotation (bars 26–7). Three bars of impetuous intensification, initially broken up by rhythm (33a) (bar 28), which continues to be related to a motive from the principal theme of the second movement. A *Generalpause* before the climax. Thereupon the arpeggiated 6–4 chord, which in that context is actually more jarring than the most extreme dissonance. Harmonic clouding and collapse, analogous to the twenty-first bar (bar 32); declamatory return of the second violin. Coda (bar 36): beginning with the third strophe's eighth rhythm, yet motivically reaching back to the beginning of the third movement – or the "new motive" of the fourth. Renewed cello intonation with rhythm (33a), unmistakable feeling of close. With the fortieth bar all rhythmic contours dissolve in the eighths, which trickle away. One instrument after another falls silent. The viola alone remains, but it is not even allowed to expire, to die. It must play for ever; except that we can no longer hear it.

Der Wein

"Claudel on Baudelaire's style: C'est un extraordinaire mélange du style racinien et du style journaliste de son temps."[1] It is very unlikely that Berg knew this excerpt from Hofmannsthal's *Buch der Freunde*. And yet one can scarcely imagine a more fitting motto for the concert aria *Der Wein*, which combines three poems from Baudelaire's cycle in a large vocal form. Allegoric melancholy and trivial frivolity; the laboriously invoked spirit of the bottle and the impudent, importunate musical commodity of the tango; the brooding sounds of the hermit's soul and the alienated conviviality of the

---

1 ["It is an extraordinary mélange of the style of Racine and the journalistic style of his era."]

piano and saxophone from a jazz or salon orchestra – with all of this the aria shapes a rebus full of the fatal significance one finds only in the language and metaphors of Baudelaire; not until *Lulu*, for which this work seems the prolegomenon, is the rebus completely clarified.

Berg the avant-gardist was intrigued by the idea of modernism as it first attained self-awareness in the poetry and theoretical writings of this poet. Newness is his central tenet, not only in "O mort, vieux capitaine," but also in the essay about Constantin Guys, whom Baudelaire elevated to the "painter of modern life." *Nouveauté* in Baudelaire combines artistic experience with childhood, in complete accord with the work of Proust fifty years later.

L'enfant voit tout en *nouveauté*; il est toujours *ivre*. Rien ne ressemble plus à ce qu'on appelle l'inspiration, que la joie avec laquelle l'enfant absorbe la forme et la couleur … Le génie n'est que l'*enfance retrouvée* à volonté, l'enfance douée maintenant, pour s'exprimer, d'organes virils et de l'esprit analytique qui lui permet d'ordonner la somme de matériaux involontairement amassée.[2]

Berg could not help being attracted by poetic works of that kind, particularly that eminently aesthetic conjunction of involuntary remembrance and conscious command, which, curiously, was ignored by both Bergson and Proust. Deeply ingrained in Berg's physiognomy is the Baudelairian will to objectify irrational subliminal enervation in a work of art through the rational energy of the ego. Few things are as noticeable in Berg as the combination of near imponderable subtlety with planning so manic that it reaches the point of number games. The oeuvre of his contemporary Valéry revolves around this same polarity; it is first operative in Baudelaire, and in his penchant for first precedents for his own ideas, Berg was as drawn to the phenomenon in Baudelaire as he was to Büchner and Wedekind.

However, Baudelaire's concept of modernity is not merely one of progressive artistic techniques, but also includes the non-aesthetic, societal reality against which those techniques are put to the test. For Baudelaire, modernity in its tangible sense is the world of commodities. According to Baudelaire's concept the artist must at once embrace that world and defend his autonomy. Already a hundred years ago, he employs in this context the

---

2 Charles Baudelaire, *L'Art romantique*, Paris 1868, p. 62. ["The child sees everything in a state of newness; he is always *drunk*. Nothing more resembles what we call inspiration than the delight with which a child absorbs form and colour […] Genius is nothing more nor less than *childhood recovered* at will, a childhood now equipped for self-expression with manhood's capacities and a power of analysis which enables it to order the mass of raw material which it has involuntarily accumulated." *The Painter of Modern Life and Other Essays* by Charles Baudelaire, translated and edited by Jonathan Mayne (Phaidon Publisher Inc.: Greenwich, 1964), 8.]

image of the *tour d'ivoire*, the ivory tower. And yet at the same time that his pathos enters that already over-populated structure, Baudelaire begins to have doubts about its historic relevance. "Je connais plusieurs personnes qui ont le droit de dire: 'Odi profanum vulgus;' mais laquelle peut ajouter victorieusement: 'et arceo?'"[3] he writes in praise of Delacroix. It was his intention to raise the commodity to the level of style by means of formal design, or, as he classicistically expressed it: "pour que toute *modernité* soit digne de devenir antiquité".[4] That was in direct correspondence to Berg's addictive tolerance for the decayed nineteenth century. He was no doubt as familiar with the Guys'ian, or rather Baudelairian passion "d'épouser la foule," to unite with the masses, as with the desire to transfigure the pictureless, anti-pictorial world of the big city into a picture, as the poet praised in Guys: "Il contemple les paysages de la grande ville, paysages de pierre caressés par la brume ou frappés par les soufflets du soleil ... Le gaz fait tache sur la pourpre de couchant."[5]

For the composer the commercial world is represented by the idiom of popular music, by the new dances of those years. Berg was not interested in learning about jazz until very late, not until 1925,[6] and held himself extremely aloof from it, in stark contrast to those versatile contemporaries who sought to adapt it to art music in hopes of finding in its false originality a corrective for the decadence of which these merry gentlemen were surely the last to be suspected. Berg was as thoroughly free from such temptation as from its philistine opposite: using jazz as a cheap symbol for a perniciousness born only of wishful phantasies. And yet he did not simply withdraw from the experience of jazz: the sound of the *Lulu* orchestra and the cloakroom scene of the first act could scarcely have been conceived without it. For years he pondered the use of the saxophone, to which he was ready in an instant to surrender. Not ready, though, to surrender to jazz. The consequences he draws takes the fun out of it. As one would later say in Brechtian terminology: those aspects are alienated and off-set through construction. *Der Wein* is not only the first time in which Berg applies the twelve-tone

---

3 *Ibid.*, p. 30. ["I know several people who have a right to say *'Odi profanum vulgus'*; but which among them can triumphantly add 'et arceo'?; "The Life and Work of Eugène Delacroix," in: Mayne, 60.]

4 *Ibid.*, p. 70. ["[...] for any 'modernity' to be worthy of one day taking its place as 'antiquity' [...]", Mayne, 13.]

5 *Ibid.*, pp. 65f. ["He gazes upon the landscapes of the great city – landscapes of stone, caressed by the mist or buffeted by the sun [...] The gas-light makes a stain upon the crimson of the sunset." Mayne, 11.]

6 The author can lay to rest any doubts about this date with his clear recollection of the evening in a Viennese bar when this occurred.

Alban Berg

technique to an entire work, it is also strictly organized as a tripartite whole: he structures the first song as a sonata exposition, the second as a kind of scherzo replacing the development section, again omitted, the third as a reprise. At the same time the work takes pains to cultivate a certain detachment, as if in tribute to dandyism. Being an aria, it belongs to the same type of performance vehicle as Berg's concertos; the vocal line is already so ingeniously denatured that it is as far removed from the essence of song as is the coloratura writing in *Lulu*. That, too, is in keeping with an aspect of Baudelaire's aesthetic: if he said that nature does not exist in the eyes of most of his contemporaries, particularly businessmen, then the poet will find it difficult to distance himself from the perceptual attitudes of the majority. Berg's virtuosically artificial concert aria captures something of that. Its posture is more one of alluding to the poems than of allowing the compositorial subject to sing *tel quel* from the heart; it is up to the listener to attune himself to this musical attitude from the outset.

Jazz, a phantasmagoria[7] of modernity, is illusory [*scheinhaft*]: counterfeit freedom. Musically this illusion is a rhythmic one: the law of the pseudo meter [*Scheintakte*]. All jazz obeys this law in a literal sense. The technical idea behind jazz could be thus defined: to handle a sustained basic meter in such a way that it appears to be constituted from differing meters without yielding anything of its rigid authority. In the tango passage of "Der Wein" (Example 34) Berg adheres faithfully to the pattern: with syncopation and shifting accents he creates the 2/4 meter by adding together two groups of three sixteenths and one of two sixteenths. The three-sixteenths pulse within a 2/4 meter creates the characteristic tango effect. Berg emphasizes that in crucial moments. Compositional intention critiques the primitive jazz habit of paralyzing the pseudo meter through off-beat accents in the large drum

Example 34

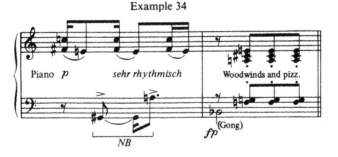

7 Cf. Baudelaire, *ibid.*, p. 67.

116

and bass line. The 2/4 meter is given its due by the placement of the barlines; however, the three sixteenths, which are a mere rhythmic façade in the tango, exact consequences. That is brought about by rhythmic counterpoint within the polyphonic texture of the whole. Berg incorporates the three sixteenths in the accompaniment in such a way that, relinquishing the bass line effect, he has the accompaniment, a G # and an A, each three sixteenths in duration, enter two sixteenths late (Example 34 NB).

Thus the melodic group 3/16 + 3/16 + 2/16 is simultaneously contrasted with its rhythmic retrograde: 2/16 + 3/16 + 3/16, thus the pseudo meter is worked out by means of a thorough development of its underlying principle; at the same time, however, the mechanism of jazz, the counterfeit integration of impotent subjectivity and inhuman objectivity, is transformed. Berg breaks his law by fulfilling it; the mechanical beats fall silent and the law itself is transformed into expression: the tango peers out of the music as with the empty eyes of a skull, symbolizing the fact that the conviviality of intoxication, of which Baudelaire's poetry speaks, is nothing but the allegorical figure of fatal estrangement. Even insanity − Baudelaire's "spleen" − is forced to give up its truth − as the "*idéal.*" Kitsch, not tastefully dismissed but rather extended by its own laws, is, under these compositional hands, transformed into style; thus the banal stands revealed as the phenomenon [*Erscheinung*] of the commodity and thus as the prevailing societal premise: but at the same time as a cipher of its downfall. Annihilation and deliverance, which Tango-kitsch undergoes in "Der Wein" − just as had vestiges of folklore in *Wozzeck* − are the paradigm for the annihilation and deliverance which Berg, a dialectician like all great artists of his historical stature, finally metes out to the human commodity: Lulu.

The aria insistently translates the trivial into style. Moreover, its relationship to translation in general is extremely close. The fact that Berg the combinatorial strategist [*Kombinationsspieler*] composed it as one great "Ossia," singable with Baudelaire's original as well as with George's translation, reveals a very significant perspective. The symbolist school, for which the aria serves as an obituary in that it bids the school dissolve its pose in the Lethe of song − this symbolist school, from Baudelaire's Poe-translations to George's free adaptation of the *Fleurs du mal* itself, cannot be understood apart from the canons of translation. This school seeks to rescue its own language from the curse of banality by viewing it from the perspective of a foreign language and paralyzing its commonplace qualities under the Gorgon-like gaze of foreignness; with respect to its language, each of Baudelaire's poems as well as each of George's must be measured according to the ideals of translation. However, in taking up the dialectic between style and banality, the prescribed escape route of symbolist procedure, Berg is communing with the ideal of translation. Through the act of translation itself kitsch actually becomes style. Not only did Berg combine the original text and its translation, but the music itself sounds as if it had been translated from the French; *Lulu* remains true to this. Granted, given Berg's point of departure, translation is used in a way diametrically opposed to its use by the neoromantics. They attempted to exorcize the banality of their own language, the *style journaliste*, by freezing it under the influence of the foreign; Berg salvages the banal appearance [*Schein*] of the foreign language by translating that appearance into his own constructive rigor and calling it by name. The aria is a twelve-tone composition, assembled out of fragments of the French musical idiom. Tolerance for tonal elements becomes coquetry with polytonality; the smallest link becomes a merging of sounds and Debussy-like *Laissez vibrer* – as exemplified by the entrance of the voice in the fifteenth and sixteenth bars; major eruptions occur three times over the ninth chord as an harmonic assortment [*Panazee*] of Impressionism.

But the form, though perhaps more fluid than anywhere else in Berg, sacrifices neither firm outline nor a tendency toward gradual harmonic development that later dominates the technique of *Lulu*. Skillfully the form permeates the schema of the tripartite song. Rather long introduction: unparalleled amalgam between melancholy and mania in the Baudelairian tradition. The principal theme of the first song section that follows, "L'Ame du vin," is based on a melodic figure in eighths and a parlando-like figure in sixteenths. By means of very discreet accent displacement and the principle of differentiation, the transition – beginning in bar 31 – prepares the syncopations of the pseudo meter. These are exposed by the piano sound leaping out of the texture in the second of the tango theme (bar 39, cf. Example 34), which is initially derived from a diminution of the transitional rhythm, but which, in order to explore the full range of banality in what follows, introduces a number of contrasting subsidiary figures: each of them in turn the derivative of a tango formula. The tango rhythm is abandoned in bar 64 and a concluding theme group established that is reminiscent of the melodic eighth-note figure of the principal theme. This theme group builds to the first climax over the ninth chord (bar 73) and is thereupon brought calmly to a rounded conclusion. Once again, as in the first movement of the *Lyric Suite*, the development section is omitted. Its place is taken by the second song, "Le Vin des amants," in the form of a scherzo. It is characterized by the dotted tritone motive of the vocal entrance and chordal catapult of triadic harmonies, reminiscent of the third variation of the Chamber Concerto. The voice formulates a contrasting idea in floating, unaccented half notes; it alternates with the actual scherzo section and at its return (bar 114) is carefully liberated from the strong beat by means of syncopated entrances;

accentuation is completely suspended. At bar 123 clear repetition of the scherzo. Then (bars 141ff.) orchestral interlude: complete retrograde of the second scherzo half. Its triplet pattern changes gradually to the eighths of the aria's introduction. – The third song, "Le Vin du solitaire," is a much varied and shortened reprise of the first. The principal theme is replaced by a combination of the introduction, the concluding theme group melody from bar 64, and the original parlando figure. This is compressed into six bars; the transitional group, even more severely, into two. The tango episode, however, returns at length. The concluding group enters immediately with the ninth chord, which in the exposition had not appeared until the climax. In bar 202 the coda begins with a sense of simplification over a pattern of repeated eighth-note chords from the tango episode. An orchestral epilogue reaches beyond the voice, which has fallen silent. Undiminished conclusion.

To this day music has hardly been a match for the secular quality of Baudelaire's poetry. With atrocious success the best-known settings, those by Henri Duparc, relegate the *Fleurs du mal* to the sphere of salon music. The five Baudelaire songs by Debussy are certainly not among his *chefs d'oeuvre*. The first song's freshness has nothing of the morbidity of its text, the whole song sounds like the piano reduction of an orchestral fragment; the last song's effeminacy is at odds with the bearing of the fencer, for which Baudelaire had a penchant; perhaps only "Le Jet d'eau" is completely fitting and masterly. Nor can Berg's aria still all doubts. The question arises whether the reasons may not lie with Baudelaire. If the phrase about a "star without atmosphere"[8] applies to him, it remains uncertain whether in the orbit of such a star music is tolerated or paralyzed. In any event Baudelaire's dialectical attitude toward Romanticism makes setting him very much more difficult; the attempt to do so will almost invariably contradict one or the other of his opposing impulses. Neoclassicism, which was flourishing during Berg's time, wanted to carry out a Baudelairian mandate, that of writing music "without a nimbus" ["*nicht auratische*" *Musik*]. That failed: modernity had to pay the price of its immanent modernity. Berg resisted that temptation. Baudelaire's fatal melancholy is exquisitely captured in the long instrumental introduction. On the other hand, Berg did not completely resist undaunted romanticization; the second song has more *neudeutsch élan vital* than anything he ever wrote, and in effect, if not in compositional means, approaches the familiar. There is also a certain unmistakable discrepancy between the finely chiselled quality of Baudelaire's verses and the interplay

---

8 Quoted by Walter Benjamin, *Schriften* I, Frankfurt 1955, p. 467.

Alban Berg

of compositional textures; in that regard Berg rarely went further than he did in the concert aria, where his goal was to incorporate the French-impressionistic idiom within his own style. Nonetheless there is more than enough in the piece that stands the test.

The last poem begins: "Le regard singulier d'une femme galante / Qui se glisse vers nous comme le rayon blanc / Que la lune onduleuse envoie au lac tremblant." Berg returned this strange gaze, which brings wild tears to the eyes of those who meet it unprotected, with a long, absorbing gaze of his own. But the purchased gaze was becoming archaic for him, just as it had for Baudelaire. For him the big city's arc-light moon seems to date from the hetaerian era. If Baudelaire defined modernity, one half of art, as "le transitoire, le fugitif, le contigent,"[9] and its other half as classically conceived objectification, then that approximates closely enough Berg's own musical complexion. Baudelaire's phrase "Le *rien* embellit ce qui est"[10] could have served as his motto. Under this sign Berg then set *Lulu*, whose composition overlapped with that of the Baudelaire poems. It needed only the spark of inspiration to bring out the radiance that lies dormant in *Der Wein*.

Experiences with *Lulu*

Since it is impossible to present what alone would be appropriate and necessary − namely, an analysis of *Lulu* of the kind necessitating a complete revision of the prevailing notions of analysis − the author will at least set out a few experiences with the work. The two essays below are separated by thirty-three years. The first consists of impressions of the 1935 London performance of the *Lulu Suite* under Sir Adrian Boult. That was the last of the author's literary works Berg read. The second is devoted to the opera itself, which the author has in the meantime heard frequently in various performances and which he has studied with the score and with Böhm's recording. There will be no attempt to bring the first spontaneous reaction in line with the conclusions resulting from long and repeated examination of the work. Through reflection, the author has attempted to come to grips with and set into context that which once struck him so forcefully. The difference between the texts may indicate something of what has in the interval happened not only to the work, but to musical awareness.

9 Baudelaire, *ibid.*, p. 69. [Baudelaire's entire sentence reads: "By 'modernity' I mean the ephemeral, the fugitive, the contingent, the half of art whose other half is the eternal and the immutable." Mayne, 13.]
10 *Ibid.*, p. 99. ["*Nothing* embellishes *something*", Mayne, 31.]

Experiences with *Lulu*

I

We will have to forego a coherent account of the *Symphonic Pieces* from the opera *Lulu*, since the work is so intimately bound up with the stage and wedded to the poetic word that it cannot be wholly grasped in isolation. That is not to say that Berg's purely compositional skill has in any way diminished. Those who know anything about his style would expect in his second opera to find music that is thoroughly structured, autonomous, and, to use a traditional word: "absolute." – And that expectation will be even more richly rewarded than in *Wozzeck*. But this construction, though far more than a mere illustration of the text-drama, is nonetheless organized around the words as around a dark kernel from which it draws its sustenance at every moment. Wordless, it stands as an inherently complete structure, yet one that is at the same time sealed off. Penetrating its secret through the music alone requires more than attending a dress rehearsal and performance and familiarity with the score: it requires years of immersion. Instead of making such pretensions it is better to note what the work has to say to the listener on first hearing – the *first* impression, which only thorough understanding can equal in importance. To begin with one must note what is *new* in *Lulu*, even measured against Berg's previous works.

Compared to *Wozzeck* there is a further conspicuous and most striking *simplification* of Berg's style: a simplicity of abundance. Nothing of the differentiation in Berg's compositional manner has been sacrificed; not the least concession made to neoclassic and old romantic tendencies; the sound is richer, certainly more radiant and colorful than the muted sound of *Wozzeck*, the harmonic language is more graduated, the counterpoint more unfettered. At the same time, paradoxically, there is an overriding impression of simplification. That is because: the new score carries the demands of *clarity* to new heights. This brings Berg into a new constellation with his roots: Mahler and Schoenberg. It is the late Mahler, to which *Lulu* is connected in so many ways, just as *Wozzeck* is to the unfathomable sorrow of the soldier in early Mahler – it is the Mahler of the Seventh and Ninth Symphonies who admonishes him not to write a single voice, a single doubling, a single note that is not absolutely clear and comprehensible from its placement and orchestration alone. With that the fore- and background of half-distinct, half-present phenomena disappear; whatever is contained in the music is immediately and completely perceptible; everything vague and shadowy is banned or, if you will, is itself brought to evidence; there is nothing the careful ear does not hear, and it is this full presence of all the music that gives the appearance of simplicity. If Krenek, proceeding from the relationship to the text, emphasized the perceptibility of the opera *Lulu*, then this is evident not only in the choice of a text that speaks more through concepts than pictures, but also in the structural qualities of a music which, like its beloved, Lulu, "never wanted to seem to be anything other" than what it was taken to be; and that is precisely why it is never taken for anything other than what it is: music whose substance is so completely at one with its appearance, as is its very object: beauty.

That suggests *technical* evolution in all regards. The Mahlerian principle of orchestration leads to a principle of construction *per se*. This principle has its corrective in Schoenberg's twelve-tone method, which Berg adapts in a most idiosyncratic manner and which is transformed by the collision with dramatic expression. To give some rough orientation one could say that *Lulu* is to *Wozzeck* as Schoenberg's Variations, Op. 31, are to the Orchestral Pieces, Op. 16, or to *Erwartung*. Except that in Berg the constructive force has an effect quite opposite to that in Schoenberg. There, construction devouringly wrests all appearance into the creation as into its very truth, while in Berg appearance greedily consumes the inherent constructive self and thus transfigures appearance to that self's truth. That can be documented: in Schoenberg's harmony book, in a passage dealing with new sonorities, he indicates that alleged dissonances lose their terrors when they are widely spaced or at least when clashing minor seconds are avoided. Schoenberg never really gave this sentence another thought and made his decisions regarding register and the spacing of dissonances solely according to constructive principles and inherent laws such as that requiring constant registral change, without any regard for their [aural] "appearance." With Berg, on the other hand, appearances themselves become the constructive principle, thereby giving Schoenberg's casual remark canonic significance for *Lulu*. Schoenberg has no compunction, even in choral settings, about using minor second clashes, whereas even in the orchestral passages of *Lulu* they are consistently avoided, or at most used for specific expressive intent. The consequence of this type of texture is an entirely fresh sound: that of an exceedingly stratified harmonic language which is continually awaiting its twelve-tone chord, indeed, lures it as Lulu does her murderer – and yet seems so free of dissonance and so sensuously euphonious that in London even the colors of Ravel's *Daphnis et Chloë* paled in comparison.

The principle of wide spacing is pervasive and produces the most extraordinary instrumental effects. At times it seems as if the instrumental texture had escaped orchestral gravity. As in one of the climaxes of the rondo, bars 128 and 129 – the Alwa music: the violins and three flutes are led fortissimo to the high G. As if the music were reaching past itself out of sheer exuberance, this climax is transcended and the next highest B laid above it. The three clarinets play it in unison. One would think that in that precarious register and pitted against the brilliance of the strings the effect of this highest note would be diminished. But the instrumental disposition of the entire passage, particularly the doubling of the lower octave by the oboes, is such that the B of the three solo instruments exceeds in radiance not only the ensemble G but the entire orchestral tutti. The indescribable effect of Lulu's death chord is similarly the result of orchestrational texture. The clarity and transparency of the orchestral sound become an expressive catalyst: never before has a twelve-note sonority been felt with such genuine penetration. For never before was such a sonority so clearly the multiplicity of unity.

The power of appearance, as reflected in clarity and textural spacing [*Setz-kunst*], characterizes the expression of the sensuously beautiful as well as the nature of *compositional* procedure. As if placed in the sunlight, the voices lay claim to the sonoral space created for them. They want to move within that space: they rise up in long arches and sing out in full. Whatever it was that could be called specifically expressionistic in the *Wozzeck* style: the isolated sound as an expressive factor – that recedes in *Lulu*: the very mastery in the manipulation of sound draws it completely into the compositional structure; its transparency allows the independent voice to be heard: as *melody*. Everything is more flexible, supple, linear. Of the *Symphonic Pieces*, only one, Lulu's Song, is a vocal piece. But to judge by that and by Countess Geschwitz's final lines at the end of the Adagio-Finale, the vocal line in *Lulu* is central throughout, the human voice carries the operatic action. Berg's new vocal style is most clearly anticipated in Marie's Cradle Song and in the middle piece of *Der Wein*. It is a melodic line of almost floating ecstasy. No longer any discrepancy between instrumental and vocal melodic style; Lulu's soprano plays in coloratura the way the violins sing. Unerring the sureness with which Berg's vocal style repudiates that Lulu whom cliché would make into an "elemental being," and seizes instead upon the child-like/artificial aspect of the character, in which her beauty and her mortality are united. One of Wedekind's stage directions requires that Lulu kiss Alwa "with deliberation"; and this seductive care shimmers over Lulu's music, the fragile coloratura as an enigma of a beauty whose nature fulfills itself in artificiality. But the contrapuntal lines wind around Lulu's music, as transparent as the clothes which the Marquis von Keith envisions for his beloved. One would almost like to think that the relationship of this music to its text is like that of clothes to the body: clothes which reveal as more beautiful that body which, naked, is shrouded by its truth.

The technical – and hence the supra-technical – evolution is most apparent in the *harmonic* language. Here the agility of the *Lulu* style leads to unexpected results. In Berg's earlier works the artistry lay in his continually modifying a basically static harmony and yet keeping everything in motion. It is no coincidence that an entire scene in *Wozzeck* is constructed on one sustained pedal and another is created out of the alternation of three sonorities. But in *Lulu* the dimension of *time* intrudes; in retrospect the conquest of the temporal dimension appears to be the real goal of the Chamber Concerto and the *Lyric Suite* as well. There is harmonic progress; adjoined to melodic plasticity is an extremely clear awareness of harmonic substructure.

That becomes outwardly apparent – as it does in later Schoenberg – in a continuo-like accompaniment of harp, piano, and vibraphone. – *Wozzeck* was conceived as with bated breath, at once eternal and of the moment, as captured in the grotesque words of the Captain; *Lulu* flows on as does life itself. The most profound insight into this aspect is revealed by Berg's calling for the "tempo of a heartbeat" for Lulu's Song. At all times the music knows within itself the lateness of the hour. To be sure, it would be irreconcilable with Berg's sense for form and understanding of appearance if the work of art were left to the mercies of the flow of time. Just as here, too, he disdains crass contrasts and unfolds the living organism in all its rich interrelationships, time is interpreted according to what happens in it, by rising and falling destiny, and is held together by that rhythm. That is why the form of the ostinato, the film music – the work's caesura and its innermost reflection – is in strict retrograde: time passes and revokes itself and nothing points beyond it but the gesture of those who love without hope.

It is scarcely necessary to state that this sense for form imposes form even upon the fragmentary publication, these five excerpts. They stand for the form of the whole, as only a large torso can. They are united into a *symphony*: it is as the *Lulu Symphony* that this first published form will become familiar. Nowhere is the relationship to late Mahler clearer than here. Five movements: the outer ones thoroughly symphonic in nature, as in Mahler's Ninth, enclose three shorter middle movements, each distinct in "character" – perhaps analogous to the Seventh Symphony. Again almost Mahlerian, the opening movement is a broad rondo with the most intricate sectionalization and at the same time extremely taut in construction; with an exalted tone that was pressaged in the Andante affettuoso of *Wozzeck* and the Trio estatico of the *Lyric Suite*, but which only now has become entirely free and unfettered. If one is looking for details there could be no more beautiful example than the very beginning, the eight introductory bars – the kind of sadness and bliss present only in the promise of beauty itself. These bars will one day be regarded as the definitive expression of the unquenchable pain that seizes us in the presence of the beautiful, just as Schumann's tone embodies loneliness amid great festivities. After that the breathless, hurried film music, as virtuosic as a career, evanescent as fireworks, stopping short midway. The middle piece, Lulu's Song, glassy clear and bright, prose of insight and poetry of the body combined in melody. The following short variations are authentic musical surrealism. Lulu's fall is crassly depicted in fallen music; a ballad by Wedekind which is scarcely varied, but covered with voices as plaster ornaments cover the ceiling of a salon; the decadence of the 1890 pop tune glows like a melancholy gaslight to Lulu's last flight. The Adagio-Finale is the death scene. Strangely enough, it is precisely this piece, on first hearing the most striking and accessible of all, which breaks the symphonic mold and compellingly calls for the stage. For the horror that lives in this music — perhaps most chilling in the horn passage of the ninety-first bar[1] — can only be borne when the eye is forewarned by the plot out of which that music arises. But then the music will be freed from the plot: free to achieve the fatal reconciliation expressed in Geschwitz's last words.

II

The opera *Lulu* is one of those works that reveals the extent of its quality the longer and more deeply one immerses oneself in it. Berg's original concept of development itself underwent development. No longer is the process one of moving from one sonority to another, from one phrase to the next, as was appropriate for the held breath, the intensified moment of Expressionism, but rather one of unfolding over long stretches. Large forms are affected by Berg's dynamism, far beyond what was possible in the compressed situations of *Wozzeck*, yet without individual details thereby losing anything of their definition. During a lesson Berg once praised a chamber work because its development section took on real momentum. This praise, whether deserved or not, can be interpreted as the expression of a compositional interest that dominated all others in the mature Berg and in *Lulu* came into its own. Here dramatic music means that the musical structures, as something evolving, are filled with the kind of tension that in *Wozzeck* was reserved for the junction points. To be sure, there are already tentative beginnings there. The doctor's passacaglia, though a bit extraterritorial in relation to its surroundings, is the nearest precursor of the later compositional technique. If in *Wozzeck* the first scene is still relatively loosely structured as a suite and only the second act takes on grand symphonic proportions, there is an analogue for that in *Lulu*: the first scene with Alwa is a compilation of short beginnings, as if the *recitativo accompagnato* had

1 All bar numbers refer to the old score of the *Five Symphonic Pieces*.

125

become a music-dramatic form in its own right. At about the same time Schoenberg had revived the use of intermittent recitative in his comic opera *Von heute auf morgen*. The very complex texture of the two operas, which were both genuine music dramas from the dramaturgic standpoint, required for the sake of their own lucidity the resurrection of that dualism between recitative and what was once called the number, which Wagner's stylistic dictatorship had abolished. At the same time Berg gives recitative, with its stops and starts and its lack of momentum, expressive function: in the first scene that of nervous embarrassment. Berg's sense for form leads him to return to the idea of recitative at the beginning of the second act, at Geschwitz's appearance; the expressive character is related.

Among the *desiderata* for the music dramatist not the least is that of inventing new expressive characters, to conquer non-musical territory for music, as Wagner first succeeded in doing in his Beckmesser music. The next model for the pieces within pieces in *Lulu* may be the grand introductory maidservants scene in *Elektra*. The economy of musical explication, which is suppressed and only takes shape, as it were, before the ears of the listener, is one means of dynamizing the whole; from a succession of beginnings to large continuous movements. Whereas in the opening scene the recitative passage is followed by relatively short, inherently closed but individual pieces, firmly defined by their basic character, the sonata exposition of the first scene between Lulu and Doctor Schön (bars 533 to 668) − scene in both senses of the word − is developed into a large dynamic form; it is directly followed by the painter's suicide scene, which unfolds like some fateful process. But such developmental forms are invariably balanced or, as in the case of the Schön sonata, repeatedly interrupted by short, lucid numbers. It is one of the polarities of *Lulu* that the work, so much more spacious than *Wozzeck*, nonetheless molds separate pieces much more distinctly than did Berg's first opera. In fact, Berg deserves the greatest admiration for the way he makes unfettered music in *Lulu* without any restrictions and yet remains ever vigilant that the dynamic forms do not crush the dramatic requirements of any given moment. Thus he structured the first scene of the second act − perhaps the *scène à faire* of the whole opera − in such a way that episodes (the unnoticed observer Schön and the underworld characters) repeatedly interrupt the rondo (Alwa's and Lulu's love duet) by means of compositional parentheses such as Boulez later cultivated in his Third Piano Sonata; in *Lulu* they create a grotesque effect and color the love scene in crass irony. Those who like to revel in the use of traditional forms will not get very far with *Lulu*, significant as their role in this opera is; they only serve to liberate Berg's formal fantasy and are constantly producing new constructions. As in *Wozzeck*, the forms are anchored in the past, through the traditional music-dramatic means of the *Leitmotif*. Most of the motives, for instance the dominating scale, beginning with a mordant, that represents Lulu's coquetry, are extremely supple and extensively varied, in other words are more connective tissue than distinctly identifiable.

The structural innovations are of greater import than the innovations of detail, of which there is no lack. It is seldom that individual sonorities are as laden with meaning as in *Wozzeck* − though when that happens, as with the twelve-tone chord of Lulu's death, it is incisive. On the other hand the over-all sound is thoroughly original, a layering of phantasmagorical brilliance over a primary base of horror. In contrast to *Wozzeck*, *Lulu*'s reputation as a singer's opera is justified by the sweeping melodic vocal lines. But performances should not make the mistake of stolidly reversing old tradition by emphasizing the voice at the orchestra's expense; if the performance does not allow the orchestra breadth and spatial depth, the work will inevitably forfeit its spiritual profundity. The individual details present fewer aural stumbling blocks than in many of Berg's earlier works. Not only because there is more of what seems like melody for the ear to hold on to. The actual melodies − thus in a Bergian way similar to Schoenberg's contemporary twelve-tone pieces − approach the traditional shape of melodic structure. That is conditioned by the principle of spinning out [*Ausspinnen*], which permits and requires the repetition of melodic elements that had been taboo in the expressionistic idiom. The Schoenberg School's tendency, which Berg never completely adopted, to work within the microstructure entirely with contrasting melodic fragments, is largely curbed in the interest of the broader line; only some of the shorter numbers employ this technique. Similarly, in addition to the use of wide registers, the harmonic language is tempered through a French quality, a suavity arising from the aim of "dein Lob zu singen, daß dir die Sinne vergehen."[2] Among *Lulu*'s most important *trouvailles*, whose full significance will probably not become apparent for some time, may be its rediscovery of the harmonic dimension, which had been rendered incidental by the contrapuntal totality of the twelve-tone system − for the work, despite its contrapuntal riches, is not composed absolutely polyphonically but attempts rather a balance between the vertical and horizontal sectors in the tradition of Viennese classicism. One should not rejoice over that particular *trouvaille* as if it meant a secret return to tonality, though, more even than in earlier works of Berg, there is no lack of tonal elements in *Lulu*. Even the concept of polytonality as it was in vogue during the heyday of *Les Six* cannot come close to a compositional process much too differentiated to be dismissed as the simple coupling of two distant

2 "To sing your praises, until your senses grow faint."

127

tonalities. At best one could speak of intensified polytonality. Chords and chordal connections are often dominant-like, layered in thirds, somewhat like ninth chords. But they are far more dissonant than ninth chords and while they contain fewer clashes between seconds, there is no lack of their octave equivalents; in addition the third formations are usually broken up, especially by additional contrapuntal lines. The Alwa passages are paradigmatic for this type of composing with a newly autonomous harmonic language. Not the least of the tasks for a patient bar-by-bar analysis would be an investigation of this new harmonic language.

Simplification of melodic characters is as much the product of *Lulu*'s compositional style as of the opera's specific sphere of expression. Berg could no more ignore the fact that the two Wedekind dramas were written in the nineties of the previous century than could a director staging the opera today. The temporal discrepancy is translated into the choice of material that is remote and estranged from the composition. That is true not only of Wedekind's ballad and presumably of much from the unpublished third act. The preceding acts, too, occasionally conjure up salon music in a way reminiscent of Max Ernst's photo montages of graphic material from the nineteenth century. Thus the theme of the strophic duettino between Lulu and the painter in the second scene of the first act (bars 416ff.) is phrased and declaimed like a chanson. The gavotte theme (first intimated in bars 561f. and then fully realized in bars 586ff.), which is fitted into the Schön sonata as a secondary theme and ultimately developed into the letter duet, sounds like an echo of all the gavottes from high-class popular music of the same period. Such reminiscences, by way of contrast, throw the darker planes into relief. These in turn are not by any means always complex; toward the end of the murder scene in the second act, as of about bar 587, there are passages with octaves and other parallel motion, perhaps drawing upon Beethoven's procedure toward the end of the long development in the first movement of the *Eroica*. The final adagio, Lulu's death, is tersely set. In moments such as the great outburst "O Freiheit" (second act, bars 1000ff.), the most radiant in the entire work, Berg simplifies in a way once thought characteristic of Schreker.

The reminiscences of salon music, which naturally never rise to the surface, but are thoroughly woven into the fabric of the music — the principal motive of the gavotte becomes one of the most important *Leitmotifs* of the entire work, that of Lulu's irresistibility, and extends far beyond the Schön complex — are dictated by the *principium stilisationis* of *Lulu*. It is the principle of the circus. The horrifying scene with Schön's murder is a sketch with grotesque clowns, who crouch behind all sorts of props and, when discovery threatens, begin to turn somersaults. In the

Experiences with *Lulu*

prologue Wedekind advertised his two pieces as "physical art," as in the circus; Rennert's production (Frankfurt 1960) was right to set the action in a circus ring. Musically the circus plays a role similar to that of the military milieu in *Wozzeck*; the fanfare with which *Lulu* begins is a terrifying intensification of the hawker of a tightrope troupe. There are sounds in the work like the ingenious orchestrations of those mechanical organs and dreamlike oversize hurdy-gurdies that once roared with metallic cacophony in the merry-go-rounds; that was the inspiration for the handling of the brass. Often trumpets carry the melody in that tone, sometimes sentimentalized. Berg composed and orchestrated into his music the sounds, at once triumphant and bleak, that surround the half-barbaric musical underworld like a mist. He takes the underworld *à la lettre* and likes to ban it, like a murkily gurgling stream, to the deepest registers of the orchestra. In Berg's hand such sounds become allegories, allegories of permanent catastrophe and at the same time of longing for what escaped cultural repression.

The circus style allows Berg to explore an inclination that had just begun to stir in *Wozzeck*, a taste for the absurd. Episodes in Schoenberg such as the Augustin passage in the trio of the F ♯ minor Quartet and some things – textually rather embarrassing – in *Pierrot* may have left their mark on him; yet Berg's strong, peculiar penchant cannot be explained through models. The nineteenth century, from whose industrial caverns processes and figures swarm, has become a frightening primeval world. Doctor Schön, that helpless ruling master, fashionably dressed in outmoded styles, could have stepped out of a family photograph of the period. Those dubious and ridiculous figures peopling his salon, who resemble him much more than he would like to think, are excretions from the subconscious of an overstuffed domestic interior. The composition reflects the aura of decay surrounding the recent past; the ether of the entire opera materializes in the shabbily luxuriant third act variations on the Wedekind song. One cannot deny the latent connection to Kurt Weill, whose music Berg did not like; on occasion Weill probably appropriated Brecht's melodic ideas the way Berg did those of Wedekind. His absurdities: for instance, that he was amused by the Captain's breathlessness in *Wozzeck* and even by the asthma – his own illness – suffered by Schigolch, whom he generally treats rather gently, requires some explanation. These absurdities have a touch of childishness: infantility, which is neutralized by revealing itself. The circus clown's phantasies are acted out. The Daumier-like caricatures of Wozzeck's tormentors already belonged to the same family. On this level, despite its profuse expansiveness, the expressionistic point of departure of the objectless subject asserts itself in *Lulu*. If that subject incorporates alienated people into itself, as if through a fissure, they nonetheless struggle in disorientation, are not entirely alive, rather, like that clever phrase by the mentally disturbed Senate President, Schreber, are "men sketched in passing" [*flüchtig hingemachte Männer*]. Absolute isolation and the consumer world, irreconcilably breaking apart, are correlates. To that subject, cast back upon its inner self, the people on the outside, who heteronomically and inexplicably impose their law upon it, seem like marionettes – no one in *Lulu* is more true to life than the surreal circus athlete. In order to endure those people, the isolated being, as if destroying himself, regresses into the years of his pre-individual existence and laughs over precisely that which causes panic in him. There was something of that quality in the expressionistic condition *per se*; it is retained in titles such as "Circus Man" and Berg objectifies it.

Opposed to this is Lulu, around whom everything turns. She represents repressed nature, its incommensurability with civilization, both the sin therein and retribution for it. But Berg would not have been a true artist if he had copied the eternally bourgeois-sanctioned antithesis: nature/anti-nature. In fact it is not Lulu who is the self out of whose perspective the music comes, but rather Alwa, who loves her. That affects the point of view of the music to its literary subject. Berg pays scarcely any attention to the cynical aspect of the text: he approaches Wedekind the way Schumann approached Heine's poems. Wedekind's technique of a dialogue of misunderstandings, whose discursiveness resists musical setting, presents problems for a composer, although the technique itself is one of situational estrangement, out of which the music develops. Music has never been suited to dialogue, with one phrase responding to the preceding; but it can string together and at the same time unite disparate elements and that is characteristic of Berg's compositional style. The numerous interpolations are marked by this intent. – Alwa's love – not the soul of the heroine, who has none – that is the focus of the music, which surrenders to that love just as the doomed artist surrenders to the beautiful woman. Nowhere is Berg more Baudelairian than in the fact that in the totality of modernity, which devours everyone, nothing is spared or glorified as natural. The victim draped by this music is itself a piece of reified world. The only utopia in Berg's work comes through reification, not through its opposite, abstraction. As body incarnate Lulu becomes the very imago of boundless joy, just as soul has its beginnings in the gaze of her "big child's eyes." Without any historic-philosophical reflection Berg, the day-dreamer, found the means for that by musically creating Lulu as a coloratura role. Her arching phrases float like birds in flight or skitter like lizards, as if subjectivity had yet to awaken; she who is at the mercy of all men is as much an instrument as her flute-inspired melodies are instrumental. Lulu's irresistibility and her inhumanness, proto-humanness, are one and the same; her relationship to Schön in the dressing room scene of the first act is reminiscent of the scene with the emperor and the witch in Hofmannsthal, except that here the witch finally wins. Perhaps it is not even in the actual coloratura passages that Berg achieved it most completely but in those puppet-like staccati sections that sound like the ones in Offenbach's *Olympia*; the first occurrence being on the word *tan-zen* [danc-ing] (first act, bar 102). While the animal trainer promises his audience that they shall see a soulless creature "tamed by human genius," the music, poised on the outermost dialectical edge, carries out this taming, Lulu's training in cultivated singing, and at the same time undermines it by making her most artificial sound an allegory of the unbridled passion which the world, at once rationalized and irrational, withholds from its wretched inhabitants.

The imago of Lulu draws its shining arc over the abyss, only to disappear into it. The old fogies were unable to resist labelling the subject with words like cesspool and gutter, which were popular Wilhelminian epithets for contemporary modernity. Berg's music also offers [the subject] salvation in that it incorporates what those abusive insults denounce. The chaotic element in Berg and his music are liberated in *Lulu* to become something more than merely psychological. The swarming region of the subconscious seethes like the sediment of society, ready to devour it. Berg's empathy embraces that stratum of repressed humanity, just as it had once embraced the paranoia of the victimized soldier. That stratum contains elements of genuine ambiguity: repression, which in its societal form bears all the marks of the mutilation it has suffered over the centuries, but also violence containing within it a destructive potential to which all the figures in the opera, including Lulu, fall victim. She herself belongs to that sphere and transcends it. But it is also the sphere of revolt, of hope that a culture caught up in repression is reaching its end. Lulu is cathartic not in the Aristotelian but rather in the Freudian sense: she dredges up what has been suppressed, looks it in the eye, makes it conscious, and brings it to justice by making herself its equal; a higher court, before which the appeal of the civilizing trial must take place. The work's brilliance, which both shares and has no equal in the eclipse of contemporary art, is the union of suppression with hope.

Opposition against *Lulu*, even from those who were close to Berg, was undoubtedly provoked by that grandiose gutter element; it is regarded as a stain upon the idea of the pure artist, an idea Berg embodied as did few of his contemporaries. The question remains whether that purity is not perhaps more genuine in not preserving itself and preferring to turn to what the tradition of affirmative culture has declared to be its polar opposite.

Alban Berg

That may well explain the vehemence of the objections against completing the instrumentation of the opera. And yet − though it would be extremely desirable for *Lulu* to assume its place in the opera houses as a complete, rounded work − the motivation of friends who stubbornly insist on preserving *Lulu* in its fragmentary state must be honored and taken seriously. The primary objection concerns the fact that incompleteness deserves respect on a metaphysical level; that he who ignores the verdict decreed by fate when Berg died in the midst of his work on the third act commits sacrilege; his death must have meaning, which is manifested in the form of the giant torso. Moreover, there are doubts as to *Lulu*'s relevance following the much-touted loosening of sexual taboos; today's concern is for social order as a whole. No one should be allowed to meddle with Berg's concept, not even with the orchestrational concept, to which no one could do justice. That which he left behind must remain just as it is, even though that certainly cannot be said of the current performances of the third act. The sketches to this act are insufficient for a satisfactory completion, while, as has now been demonstrated for years, the work is viable as it is; indeed, some have considered its involuntarily shortened form to be preferable.

All of the above sounds both plausible and honorable. But there are valid responses to be made. The argument that searches for meaning in the fact that Berg was unable to complete the orchestration does indeed open a metaphysical perspective; the question, however, should not be left to the ever-popular philosophical choice but can be objectively decided. One needs only say:

After Auschwitz, our feelings resist any claim of the positivity of existence as sanctimonious, as wronging the victims; they balk at squeezing any kind of sense, however bleached, out of the victims' fate. And these feelings do have an objective side after events that make a mockery of the construction of immanence as endowed with a meaning radiated by an affirmatively posited transcendence. Such a construction would affirm absolute negativity and would assist in ideological survival − as in reality that negativity survives anyway, in the principle of society as it exists until its self-destruction. The earthquake of Lisbon sufficed to cure Voltaire of the theodicy of Leibniz, and the visible disaster of the first nature was insignificant in comparison with the second, social one, which defies human imagination as it distills a real hell from human evil.[3]

Divine will and other such theological categories that are applicable to living beings are not simply transferable to art works or artefacts. No opera,

---

3 Theodor W. Adorno. *Negative Dialectics*, trans. E. B. Ashton (New York: Continuum Publishing Company, 1973), 361.

even one of the most exalted stature, is a holy text. The stature of Berg's opera, the truth it contains, demands that it not be treated − in accordance with the art religion of the nineteenth century − as if it were revelation.

Nor can *Lulu* be accused of any lack of relevance. Sexual liberation has taken place only on the façade of a still unfree and patriarchal society. While it is said that what was once called the sexual question is now dated, the continuing pain of the old wound resists being touched. No one knew that better than *Lulu*'s patron saint, Karl Kraus. Sexuality remained the point on which society, regardless of its political system, refused to jest, and that has been branded into artistic experience. To be sure, Lulu is not, as a communist dogmatist once piously imagined, the proletarian girl, victimized by the bourgeoisie, who supports her starving family with her body. But societal repression over thousands of years has been concentrated in the ambivalent relationship to female sexuality. When this sexuality, without political consciousness or manifest social motivation, collides with society, then objectively it really does become a political issue *par excellence*.

Nor is there any validity to an aesthetic objection, voiced by friends such as Hermann Scherchen: that *Lulu*, a traditional opera, is *passé*. If *Lulu* is indeed a traditional opera, then, together with Schoenberg's *Moses und Aron*, [it is] surely the last. But that is the same as saying it effects a complete shift. In this one opera, it is as if opera were gazing at itself in a mirror, itself becoming thematic, as does the nineteenth century during which time the operatic form, along with the novel, occupied a key position; not incidentally, one of the principal figures in Berg's version of the text is a composer and one of the central scenes takes place behind the scenes in a theater, though without the work falling into the fatal collection of "artist" operas. The completely sovereign command over the operatic genre amounts to its attaining self-awareness and shedding the self-conscious and accepted naiveté that historically has condemned traditional opera.

As to Berg's own subjective wishes or how he would have regarded posthumous instrumentation, this can only be pure speculation. However, he was too thoroughly convinced of the objectivity of artistic creation, differentiated too strictly between right and wrong, not to have considered independently of his own private existence the possibility of a stranger's completing the already largely completed work. Terrible as was the blow that befell him in the final phase of his work, equally strong must have been his longing to see the work completed; this is reinforced by reports of his last feverish phantasies, in which he continued to be preoccupied with the orchestration.

The strongest argument cited by opponents of orchestrating what exists only in short score is that important composers who were Berg's friends:

Schoenberg, Webern, Krenek, probably Zemlinsky, too, all declined to undertake the project. However, in an artistic question of such significance individual authority can scarcely be granted the last word. The reasons for Schoenberg's refusal were not musical, but rather such as, while understandable and by all means to be respected, resulted from a misunderstanding of Berg's point of view: that refusal is too much the expression of the wretched intrinsic confusion of the Hitler era to be binding after so many long decades. What Schoenberg objected to could be easily remedied. Webern probably feared the responsibility as much as the burden he would have had to assume. When, after his inspired orchestration of Bach's *Ricercare*, it was suggested that he complete and orchestrate the *Art of the Fugue*, he replied that it would mean giving up composing for the rest of his life; he would have felt no differently about *Lulu*. As for Krenek, even without knowing his reasons, one could imagine that he considered his own compositional as well as orchestrational style too unlike Berg's to allow him to tackle *Lulu*. Finally, Zemlinsky was so pre-Schoenbergian as a composer that, for all his solidarity, he had no choice but to acknowledge his unsuitability. At a certain temporal distance, which permits a more unencumbered perspective, the entire complex should look different.

Completion, so it seems to one who has not seen the short score, is not completely impossible. Approximately one third of the act is in full score; the short score presumably also contains orchestrational indications of the kind composers usually note down as an aid to memory. Given that Berg reported the actual composition completed, it would be most peculiar in a twelve-tone work, whose continuity always presupposes use of the entire row continuum, if the musical texture of the short score remained incomplete; it is difficult to continue a twelve-tone composition until the preceding twelve-tone bar has been fully composed. If, on the other hand, some auxiliary and accompanimental voices are indeed missing, which is not implausible in view of Berg's free application of the technique, it ought to be possible for someone well versed in Berg's style to add them convincingly, considering that these voices must necessarily have their function within the existing twelve-tone structure. *Lulu* contains paradigms for orchestrating the remaining material, particularly in the technique of instrumental variation found in the Alwa music. Berg was just at the point of completely reorchestrating several more or less literally repeated passages. That would be the way to proceed. Those who are satisfied with the present solution are hearing the composer's biographical fate in the music. But the work is separate from its author. It is insufficiently represented in the version that has meanwhile become accepted. Of all the genres, surely opera, if only because of the large acoustic space its sound requires, cannot be conceived apart from its audience. An audience that enters a theater without any knowledge of the circumstances could not help being disappointed by the present third act, sensing that in the expedient something was being denied it. That applies as much to the stylistic discrepancy — the disproportionate dominance of instrumental over vocal passages in the attic scene — as to the dramaturgic gap caused by the omission of the Casti-Piani scene. But most important: *Lulu* is rigorously constructed not only as a twelve-tone piece, but also in the over-all form; Willi Reich once correctly pointed out that many of Berg's works owe their compelling quality in part to their geometric proportions. If these proportions are ignored by performing something incomplete, then everything is thrown off balance: here respect for the existent object violates the object itself; the unity of the structure. Comparisons with the [Schubert] B minor Symphony are irrelevant.

Completing the orchestration would unquestionably require an extraordinary effort: an absolute balance of loyalty and the imagination that loyalty demands. It would probably only be possible for a collective; the orchestrators would have to criticize and correct each other, preferably by working together in one place, in a "composition-studio." It should be done soon: while the Bergian tradition is still current and while several people are still alive who know from training and personal experience what the completed *Lulu* should look and sound like. Were it to succeed, music would be given Alban Berg's greatest work.

About the text

"Tone" is a slightly revised essay, which was first published in *Kontinente* in 1955 in Vienna and which was reprinted in the *Beiträge 1967*, published by the Österreichische Gesellschaft für Musik, after being presented by the South German Radio, Stuttgart, on 24 April 1960 during the "Tage zeitgenössischer Musik."

"Reminiscence" was written in 1968, based on the essay "Erinnerungen an den Lebenden" in the issue of *23* dedicated to Berg (published in 1936 under the pseudonym Hektor Rottweiler), as well as on extensive unpublished notes from the year 1956.

In the section "The works," "Analysis and Berg" was written in 1968. The author took the following from his contributions to the 1937 book published by Willi Reich: the analyses of the Piano Sonata, the Op. 2 Songs, the Seven Early Songs, the String Quartet, Op. 3, the Clarinet Pieces, Op. 4, the Orchestral Pieces, Op. 6, and the *Lyric Suite*. The texts were edited only where deemed absolutely necessary by the author; the general character remained unchanged and nothing substantial was added.

The author was no longer satisfied with his theoretical remarks on *Der Wein* in Reich's book. He also took into account various criticisms Walter Benjamin leveled at the chapter during a conversation in 1937. The author has therefore subjected it to a complete revision while retaining the purely musical passages. Above all he wished to avoid the pretentions which the old version set up without doing them justice.

Ernst Krenek had discussed the Altenberg Songs in the Reich book; that is why the author has added his own chapter on that subject.

"Characteristics of *Wozzeck*" goes back to an essay written for the program book of the Cologne Opera during the 1958/59 season. Excerpts from the author's review of the *Wozzeck* score, published in the *Frankfurter Allgemeine Zeitung* in April 1956, have been incorporated.

The "Epilogomena to the Chamber Concerto" (1968) is completely new.

About the text

Part I of "Experiences with *Lulu*" is also based on an essay, "Zur *Lulusymphonie*," published under the pseudonym Hektor Rottweiler in the 1936 memorial issue of *23*; Part II, which was written last, is again from 1968. The author included ideas from a speech he gave at the 1960 Frankfurt premiere of *Lulu* under Georg Solti.

The Violin Concerto is not discussed because there is an extensive interpretational analysis of the work published in the author's *Der getreue Korrepetitor* (Frankfurt, 1963), which deals in detail with its idiosyncracies and compositional problems of structure.

Afterword

The following annotations make no pretense to being comprehensive. Rather, we as editors and translators have sought merely to amplify Adorno's often cryptic references with factual information gleaned from the author's other writings on Berg, or from sources relevant to their relationship. Beyond that, we have provided a few references that might not be familiar to English-speaking readers. Specific works are not annotated unless Adorno's reference is unclear or the date of a performance might be of interest; individuals are identified briefly in the index. Published Adorno sources are identified by Roman and Arabic numbers in parentheses, which refer to the relevant volume and page of the edition of Adorno's collected works (Theodor W. Adorno, *Gesammelte Schriften*, Frankfurt: Suhrkamp Verlag, 1970–1986), hereafter "GS". Reference is to page numbers in the text.

Preface

p. xvii   It is clear from his correspondence with Helene Berg (Berg Fonds, Austrian National Library) that Adorno regarded Hans Ferdinand Redlich's 1957 Berg biography (*Alban Berg: Versuch einer Würdigung*, Vienna: Universal Edition, 1957) as the principal legitimization for publishing his own Berg book. It was Redlich, according to Adorno, who in the 1930s compromised his political integrity by extolling the virtues of folk music, and Redlich who wrote an essay entitled "Der grosse Einsame," portraying Schoenberg as a "great isolated figure."

Willi Reich's Berg book of 1937, *Alban Berg* (Wien/Leipzig/Zurich: Herbert Reichner Verlag, 1937) contained contributions by Krenek on Op. 4 and by Adorno (at that time Wiesengrund-Adorno) on Opp. 1–3, 5–6, the Seven Early Songs, the *Lyric Suite*, and *Der Wein*.

p. xviii   In the first scene of Act II of Wagner's *Götterdämmerung* it is actually Alberich who entreats his son to remain loyal, "Sei treu, Hagen, mein Sohn! / Trauter Helde, sei treu!" In his "Erinnerung an den

Lebenden,'' as well as in his *Klangfiguren* essay, ''Alban Berg,'' where he cites the same scene in a different context, Adorno makes the proper attribution to Alberich (GS XVI/91).

Chapter 1: Tone

p. 7   This chapter, based on a 1955 essay, was of course written at a time when the feasibility of completing the third act of *Lulu* was still a hotly debated issue. The task was ultimately undertaken by the Austrian composer Friedrich Cerha, and the three-act version of the opera was given its first performance in Paris in 1979.

p. 8   Adorno's reference to Berg's ''bright-eyed, bushy-tailed'' (*frisch-fröhliche*) contemporaries describes the musicians associated with such 1920s movements as *Neue Sachlichkeit* (New Objectivity), Neoclassicism, and *Gebrauchsmusik* (Music for Use).

On Berg's fifteenth birthday his friend Hermann Watznauer presented him with a copy of *Das goldene Buch der Musik*, a general reference book on music. According to Berg's own account, this book provided him with his first introduction to music theory.

Chapter 2: Reminiscence

''Reminiscence'' is the last and longest of four related essays in which Adorno set down recollections and reflections about his teacher. The first, ''Erinnerung an den Lebenden,'' was published in 1936 in the Alban Berg memorial issue of the periodical *23*. In October 1955 Adorno expanded his article in an essay entitled ''Im Gedächtnis an Alban Berg,'' a manuscript that bore the proviso that it not be published ''until all who are directly or indirectly concerned have died.'' A variant of these essays, ''Alban Berg,'' was published in *Klangfiguren* (1959). Of the four essays, ''Reminiscence'' is perhaps the most carefully crafted and certainly the most lyrical. It is at the same time marked by omissions and ambiguities typical of Adorno, including the tactful suppression of names (many of which were nonetheless clearly identifiable by the informed reader). Though it would lead too far afield to detail all the differences between these sources, the following notes provide a compendium of the material relevant to the text of ''Reminiscence.''

p. 9   In ''Im Gedächtnis an Alban Berg'' Adorno identified the local comedian with whom Berg might be confused as Armin Berger. The critic who would eulogize ''the bard of *Wozzeck*'' was Paul Stefan (GS XVIII/501).

p. 9 The story of the anonymous blood donor was first told by Willi Reich. Research by George Perle and Douglas Jarman has identified the donor as Leonhard Kuhmärker (b. 1910), a Berg student who published under the name Leonhard K. Märker (in the United States he became Leonard Marker) and was in fact a composer of operettas.

p. 10 It is interesting that in his 1936 "Erinnerung an den Lebenden" Adorno simply described Berg remarking: "Only when composing do I think I'm Beethoven; never afterward." In the margin of her copy of Adorno's article (Berg Fonds, Austrian National Library) Helene Berg wrote: "He always said such things laughingly – jokingly!" Adorno's 1968 revision of this passage may have taken into account her objections to the original formulation.

p. 10 The premiere of *Wozzeck* took place on 14 December 1925.

p. 10 Webern conducted two performances of Mahler's Eighth Symphony on 18 and 19 April 1926, one of which Adorno heard during a visit to Vienna.

p. 11 It is well known that Berg was fascinated by numerology and convinced that the number 23 had special significance for him. In his last days in the hospital he feared the approach of 23 December and was visibly relieved when told that it had passed; he died in the early hours of the 24th.

p. 11 In "Erinnerung an den Lebenden" Adorno states that Berg was aware of his physical similarity to Oscar Wilde, to which Helene Berg adds in the margin of her copy of the article, "it made him angry when he was reminded of it."

p. 11 In "Im Gedächtnis an Alban Berg" Adorno claims that it was Berg who cured him of his assimilationist arrogance against Eastern Jews (GS XVIII/501).

p. 12 *Die Fackel* ("The Torch"), the satirical periodical which appeared 1899–1936, was edited and largely written by Karl Kraus.

p. 12 Berg's eldest brother, Hermann (1872–1921), emigrated to America in 1888.

p. 13 (see also p. 22) With "the first great Schoenberg scandal" Adorno is referring to the 31 March 1913 Vienna concert organized by Erhard Buschbeck and conducted by Schoenberg, in which a program of works by Webern, Zemlinsky, Schoenberg, Berg, and Mahler could not be finished because of the uproar occasioned by the premiere of two of Berg's Op. 4 Altenberg Songs (see also page 00). While it may be the best known "Schoenberg scandal" it was by no means the first.

p. 13 The mutual acquaintance was Erwin Stein, whose wife came from the north German province of Mecklenburg (GS XVIII/489f.). In "Im Gedächtnis an Alban Berg" Adorno goes on to write:

Stein was very short, even dwarf-like, his wife exceptionally tall, and Berg loved to make up love scenes between the two, in which the lady's fluting Mecklenburgian dialect played a prominent part. It boggles the mind to think what he would have done, had he lived to see their daughter marry into the English royal family and become Lady Harewood. Incidentally, he never trusted Stein; with justification, as became apparent much later, for after emigrating Stein became a standard-bearer for Benjamin Britten.

p. 13 The Berlin restaurant in question was named Schloss; in "Im Gedächtnis an Alban Berg" Adorno claims that Berg associated the restaurant, which he considered very bad, with his German student of the same name (GS XVIII/489).

p. 13 The premiere of the *Three Excerpts from Wozzeck* took place at a Frankfurt festival of new music on 15 June 1924. Adorno erroneously attributes the sponsorship of this municipally organized festival to the German composers' association, the Allgemeiner Deutscher Musikverein.

p. 13 According to his correspondence with Berg, it was not until March 1925 that Adorno arrived in Vienna.

p. 13 Berg's Hietzing address, Trauttmansdorffgasse 27, is today the headquarters of the Alban Berg Stiftung. The Berg apartment has been preserved essentially as Berg knew it.

p. 14 In "Im Gedächtnis an Alban Berg" Adorno compares his experience with Nietzsche's first visit to Wagner in Triebschen, when the philosopher heard the composer at work on a dissonant passage from *Siegfried* (GS XVIII/487). The passage in question was from Act III of the opera, where Brünnhilde sings, "Verwundet hat mich, der mich erweckt."

p. 14 Adorno likewise calls attention to similarities with Thomas Mann's *Doktor Faustus* protagonist Adrian Leverkühn in "Im Gedächtnis an Alban Berg," emphasizing in particular Berg's love of numerology and secret programs such as that of the *Lyric Suite* (GS XVIII/491). Undoubtedly many of these similarities reflect the influence of Adorno, who advised Mann on musical and aesthetic aspects of his novel.

p. 15 Berg's "not very talented student" is identified in "Im Gedächtnis an Alban Berg" as Julius Schloss (GS XVIII/489).

p. 16 References to Berg's "sensuous sensibility" are greatly expanded in "Im Gedächtnis an Alban Berg." In a passage on Berg's relationship to sex and sensuality (translated in Mosco Carner, *Alban Berg: The Man and the Work*, London: Duckworth, 1983, 66f.). Adorno states that Berg had numerous love affairs. It is here that he discusses Berg's relationship with Hanna Fuchs-Robettin and her role in the genesis of the *Lyric Suite*.

p. 16 Black and gold were the colors of the Austrian monarchy.

p. 16 In her comments on "Erinnerung an den Lebenden" Helene Berg questioned Adorno's observation that Berg spoke and wrote often about himself.

p. 17 "The poet speaks" is a reference to the title of the last piece of Robert Schumann's *Kinderszenen*, Op. 15.

p. 18 Im "In Gedächtnis an Alban Berg" Adorno states only that Freud was unable successfully to treat Berg's cold (GS XVIII/492).

p. 18 There were concrete reasons for Berg's "train complex." While traveling from Vienna to Berlin in 1929, Berg and his wife were involved in a train collision in which there were several fatalities.

p. 19 Adorno had emigrated to England in 1934.

p. 19 Karl Binder (1894–1917) was the younger brother of Maria Schreker; he died in World War I. In "Im Gedächtnis an Alban Berg" Adorno states that it was Berg himself who pointed out the Schreker parody in *Wozzeck* (GS XVIII/498).

p. 19 The use of *jugendbewegter* as an adjective recalls the *Jugendbewegung*, or *Youth Movement* of the 1920s and 30s, which in this context carries decidedly reactionary overtones.

p. 20 In "Im Gedächtnis an Alban Berg" Adorno goes into somewhat greater detail concerning Berg's friendship with Paul von Klenau, asserting that Berg saw a good deal of the Danish composer and conductor, but had only disdain for him as a musician and was amused by Klenau's anachronistically Bohemian lifestyle (GS XVIII/507).

p. 21 In margin notes in her copy of "Erinnerung an den Lebenden," Helene Berg wrote, beside Adorno's assertion that Berg was drawn to the prose of Marcel Proust, "not true."

p. 23 The German philosopher Max Scheler, with whom Adorno was associated at the University in Frankfurt, was paraphrasing Goethe's last words: "Mehr Licht" (more light).

p. 23 In "Erinnerung an den Lebenden" Adorno refers only to Berg's admiration of Hindemith's musical facility, to which Helene Berg remarked in the margin of her copy of the article: "As a person Berg liked Hindemith very much." She may have induced Adorno to add the phrase regarding "friendly contact."

p. 24 *Anbruch* was the house periodical of the Viennese music publisher, Universal Edition; Berg's analysis of Robert Schumann's "Träumerei" was contained in his article "Die musikalische Impotenz der 'neuen Ästhetik' Hans Pfitzners," which appeared in *Anbruch* II/11–12 (June 1920), 399–408.

p. 24 There is no mention of any sketches for choruses to texts of Pierre de Ronsard in the catalogue of Berg's musical legacy in the Austrian National Library.

Afterword

p. 24   In his *Klangfiguren* article, "Alban Berg," Adorno likewise speaks of Berg's use of the term "jovial," which Adorno associates with Berg's attitude toward being alive:

[...] as if the living subject felt something of the injustice caused solely by the fact that it is alive, because it is stealing life from other life, wherefore it prefers to give itself up rather than participate further in the theft. Among Berg's favorite words was jovial, and in using it he did not mean petty comfort and coziness but rather the above gesture.   (GS XVI/89)

p. 25   In "Im Gedächtnis an Alban Berg" Adorno is more direct regarding Berg's "autobiographical secrets" and briefly discusses details of the program for the *Lyric Suite* (GS XVIII/491).

p. 26   In "Im Gedächtnis an Alban Berg" Adorno implies that Soma Morgenstern had in fact argued *against* Berg's composition of Gerhart Hauptmann's *Und Pippa tanzt* (GS XVIII/503).

p. 27   Hugo von Hofmannsthal's last major tragedy, *Der Turm* ("The Tower"), was first published in installments in the Munich literary periodical *Neue Deutsche Beiträge* in 1923 and 1925; a revised version appeared in 1927. In a letter to Ernst Krenek of 5 November 1934 Adorno discusses at length his attraction to the play (*Theodor W. Adorno und Ernst Krenek Briefwechsel*, ed. Wolfgang Rogge, Frankfurt a. M.: Suhrkamp Verlag, 1974).

p. 27   The composer Ernst Krenek returned to Vienna in 1928 and adopted the twelve-tone technique around 1930.

p. 27   Stein's article on twelve-tone method was "Neue Formprinzipien," *Anbruch* VI/8 (September 1924), 286–303.

pp. 27f.   In "Im Gedächtnis an Alban Berg" Adorno identified the two composers as Egon Wellesz (who had studied with Schoenberg) and Ernst Toch. Adorno's formulation (and hence our translation) is ambiguous; in the 1955 article it is clear that Berg found Toch worse, whereas Adorno thought Wellesz the lesser composer; Adorno adds that Berg would probably have come to agree with him (GS XVIII/493).

p. 28   Berg's article on Pfitzner is cited above.

p. 28   The periodical *23. Eine Wiener Musikzeitschrift*, modeled on Kraus's *Die Fackel* and named for the press paragraph of the Austrian Civil Code, was founded and edited by Willi Reich 1932–1937.

p. 28   Adorno is referring to Stravinsky's *Three Japanese Lyrics*, completed in 1913.

p. 28   Webern conducted Bruckner's Seventh Symphony in London on 3 May 1936.

p. 29   In August 1924 Arnold Schoenberg married Gertrud Kolisch, who twenty-four years his junior. She was the sister of the violinist Rudolf Kolisch.

p. 29   Mödling, a small town south of Vienna, had been Webern's principal home since 1918. In August 1932 (after a few months' stay in Vienna) he and his family moved to the neighboring community of Maria Enzersdorf.

p. 29   Webern conducted Bruckner's Mass in F minor in Mödling's St. Othmar Church on 10 May 1925.

p. 31   In 1925 Berg began receiving from Universal Edition fixed monthly advances of 500 Austrian Schillings (eventually raised to 1,000 Schillings). U.E.'s financial difficulties after 1933 forced drastic cuts of expenditure and in Berg's last two years he received only 1,000 Schillings annually.

p. 31   Berg purchased a Ford Cabriolet in 1930; the automobile is still in working order and maintained by the Alban Berg Stiftung at the Berg property on the Wörthersee.

p. 31   Sale of the *Lyric Suite* manuscript is discussed in Adorno's correspondence with Berg beginning in March 1935. Among those mentioned as possible purchasers were the English art patron and Glyndebourne Opera founder John Christie, as well as the Swiss art patron Hans Reinhart and his brother, the conductor Werner Reinhart.

p. 31   Both here and in "Im Gedächtnis an Alban Berg" Adorno confuses the Berghof, an Ossiachersee property that had once been in the possession of the Berg family, with the "Waldhaus," the property on the Wörthersee which Berg and his wife purchased in 1932.

p. 34   The incident, in which Berg rescued a man from the subway rails, occurred in 1925 during rehearsals for the premiere of *Wozzeck*. Newspaper accounts documented the event.

Adorno's principal writings on Berg (chronologically ordered)

"Alban Berg. Zur Uraufführung des *Wozzeck*," *Musikblätter des Anbruch* VII/10 (December 1925), 531–537; XVIII/456–464.

"Alban Bergs frühe Lieder," *Anbruch* XI/2 (February 1929), 90–92; XVIII/465–468.

"Berg: Sieben frühe Lieder," *Die Musik* XXI/10 (July 1929), 761–762; XVIII/469–471.

"Die Oper *Wozzeck*," *Der Scheinwerfer. Blätter der Städtischen Bühnen Essen* III/4 (November 1929), 5–11; GS XVIII/472–479.

"Berg und Webern," (1930) *Österreichische Musikzeitschrift* XXXIX/6 (June 1984), 290–295; GS XX/782–792; published in English translation as: "Berg and Webern – Schönberg's Heirs," *Modern Music* VIII/2 (January/February 1931), 29–38; GS XVIII/446–455.

"Zum Rundfunkkonzert vom 8. April 1931" (*Der Wein*), unpublished until GS XX/793–796.

"Berg: Drei Stücke aus der Lyrischen Suite für Streichorchester," (1934 lecture), unpublished until GS XX/797–801.

"Erinnerung an den Lebenden," Sonderheft "Alban Berg zum Gedenken," *23. Eine Wiener Musikzeitschrift* 24/25 (1 February 1936), 19–29; not in GS.

"Berg-Gedenkkonzert im Londoner Rundfunk," (1936) unpublished until GS XX/802–803.

"Konzertarie *Der Wein*," (Willi Reich, *Alban Berg. Mit Bergs eigenen Schriften und Beiträgen von Theodor Wiesengrund-Adorno und Ernst Krenek* (Wien/Leipzig/Zürich: Herbert Reichner Verlag, 1937), 101–106; GS XIII/509–514. The other Adorno contributions are not republished in GS.

"Zum Rundfunkkonzert vom 11. Juni 1940," (introduction to the Piano Sonata, Op. 1, as well as works by Mahler and Wolpe), unpublished until GS XVIII/581–583.

"Für Alban Berg," *Die Neue Rundschau* LXII/1 (1951), 134–136; GS XVIII/483–486.

"Alban Bergs Kammerkonzert," (April 1954 lecture), *Musik-Konzepte 9: Alban Berg, Kammermusik II*, (Munich 1979), 54–62; GS XVIII/630–640.

Adorno's principal writings on Berg

"Im Gedächtnis an Alban Berg," (October 1955), unpublished until GS XVIII/ 487–512.

"*Wozzeck* in Partitur," *Frankfurter Allegemeine Zeitung* (18 April 1956); GS XVIII/480–482.

"Alban Berg," *Klangfiguren* (Frankfurt a.M.: Suhrkamp, 1959), 121–137; GS XVI/85–96.

"Die Instrumentation von Bergs frühen Liedern," *Klangfiguren* (Frankfurt a.M.: Suhrkamp, 1959), 138–156; GS XVI/97–109.

"Rede über Alban Bergs *Lulu*," *Frankfurter Allgemeine Zeitung* (19 January 1960); GS XVIII/645–649.

"Bergs *Lulu*-Symphonie," *Melos* (1960), 43–46; not in GS.

"Alban Berg: Violinkonzert," *Der getreue Korrepetitor. Lehrschriften zur musikalischen Praxis* (Frankfurt a.M.: Suhrkamp, 1963), 187–216; GS XV/ 338–368.

"Bergs kompositionstechnische Funde," *Quasi una fantasia* (Frankfurt a.M.: Suhrkamp, 1963), 245–273; GS XVI/413–432.

Berg. Der Meister des kleinsten Übergangs (Vienna: Verlag Elisabeth Lafite / Österreichischer Bundesverlag, 1968); GS XIII/321–496.

"Alban Berg: Oper und Moderne," (1969 lecture), unpublished until GS XVIII/ 650–672.

Index

Identification and/or dates are given only for lesser-known and twentieth-century historical figures. Italicized page references refer to the translators' introduction, notes, and afterword.

Index

Beethoven, Ludwig van, *xiii*, 10, 29, 37, 112, *140*
Eroica Symphony, 128
String Quartet in F minor, Op. 95, 29
Benjamin, Walter (1892–1940), German cultural philosopher; friend of Adorno, 14, 25, 33, 74, 119n, 136
Berg, Alban (1885–1935)
WORKS (chronologically ordered):
Seven Early Songs, *xiii*, 8, 49–53, 55, *138*; No. 1, "Nacht" (Hauptmann), 50, 52; No. 2, "Schilflied" (Lenau), 50; No. 3, "Die Nachtigall" (Storm), 50; No. 4, "Traumgekrönt" (Rilke), 50; No. 5, "Im Zimmer" (Schlaf), 50; No. 6, "Liebesode" (Hartleben), 50; No. 7, "Sommertage" (Hohenberg), 50
Piano Sonata, Op. 1, 40–46, 47, 48, 49, 50, 51, 52, 53, 54, 55, 56, 68, 72, 107–108, *138*
Four Songs, Op. 2, 47–49, 50, 55, 72, 138; No. 1, "Schlafen, schlafen" (Hebbel), 48; No. 2, "Schlafend trägt man mich" (Mombert), 48; No. 3, "Nun ich der Riesen stärksten überwand" (Mombert), 47, 48–49; No. 4, "Warm die Lüfte" (Mombert), 22, 49, 69, 71
String Quartet, Op. 3, *xi*, 22, 53–62, 68, 72, 74, 106, 109, *138*; Langsam, 55–59, 62, 74; Mässige Viertel, 22, 54, 55, 59–62
Altenberg Songs, Op. 4, 22, 62–67, 72, 136, *138, 140*; No. 1, "Seele, wie bist du schöner," 63–65; No. 2, "Sahst du nach dem Gewitterregen," 64, 65, 67; No. 3, "Über die Grenzen des All," 64, 65–66, 67; No. 4, "Nichts ist gekommen," 64, 65, 66–67; No. 5, "Hier ist Friede," 63, 64, 67
Clarinet Pieces, Op. 5, 24, 67–71, 72, 74, 76, 104, 106, 111, *138*; No. 1, Mässig, 69–70; No. 2, Sehr langsam, 70–71; No. 3,

Sehr rasch, 71; No. 4, Langsam, 71, 76, 111
Three Pieces for Orchestra, Op. 6, 22–23, 65, 72–84, 110, *138*; Präludium, 72, 73, 76–79, 110; Reigen, 73, 75, 76, 79–82; March, 22, 23, 72, 73, 74–75, 76, 79, 82–84
Wozzeck, Op. 7, *x, xi*, 5–6, 9, 10, 14, 15, 17, 19, 23, 24, 25–26, 30, 31, 33, 36, 45, 47, 48, 49, 50, 51, 68, 71, 76, 78, 79, 84–88, 89, 92n, 94, 96, 98, 104, 108, 117, 121, 122, 123, 124, 125, 126–127, 129, *138, 139, 140, 142, 144*; Wozzeck, 5–6, 10, 49, 68, 84, 86, 87, 88, 104, 129; Marie, 6, 30, 51, 71, 88, 123; Captain, 19, 68, 87, 124, 129; Doctor, 87, 125
Three Excerpts from *Wozzeck*, *ix*, 13, 141
Chamber Concerto, 14, 23, 36, 67, 88–103, 105, 107, 110, 116, 118, 124; Variations, 92, & n, 93, 95–96, 99, 100, 102, 118; Adagio, 66, 92n, 95, 96, 97–98, 99–103, 110; Rondo, 23, 36, 92 & n, 95, 96, 99, 100–103, 105, 107
"Schließe mir die Augen beide" (Storm), 106, 107
Lyric Suite, *xiiin*, 1, 28, 31, 48, 53, 56, 65, 66, 71, 81, 101, 103, 104–113, 118, 124, 138, *141, 143, 144*; Allegretto gioviale, 56, 101, 105, 106, 107–108, 118; Andante amoroso, 105, 106, 107, 108–109, 110, 111, 113; Allegro misterioso, 65, 105, 106, 107, 109–110, 111, 113, 124; Adagio appassionato, 71, 105, 106, 107, 110–112, 113; Presto delirando, 105, 106, 107, 112; Largo desolato, 105, 106, 107, 112–113
Der Wein, 12, 24, 48, 99, 113–120, 123, *138*; "L'Ame du vin," 116–117, 118, 119; "Le Vin des amants," 99, 116, 118–119, 123; "Le Vin du solitaire," 116, 119, 120
Lulu, 6, 7, 9, 12, 17, 19, 21, 22,

Index

Index

Index

Mann, Thomas (1875–1955), German novelist; Adorno advised Mann on musical aspects of his novel *Doktor Faustus*, 34, *141*
Doktor Faustus, 14, 63, *141*;
   Adrian Leverkühn, 14, 63, *141*
march, march forms, 6, 13, 58, 59, 73–74, 75, 76, 82–83, 88
Maria Enzersdorf, town in Lower Austria, 29, *144*
Marker, Leonard (Leonhard Kuhmärker, Leonhard K. Märker), Austrian-American composer, student of Berg, 140
Mayne, Jonathan, 114n, 115n, 120n
Mecklenburg, north German province, *140–141*
Metzger, Heinz-Klaus (b. 1932), German music theorist and editor, 36
Mödling, town in Lower Austria, 29, *144*
Mombert, Alfred (1872–1942), German poet, 22, 69, 71
Moravec, Rosemary Hilmar, *xin*
"Dr. Adorno war nur ein Schüler von Alban Berg," *xin*
Morgenstern, Soma (1891–1976), Austrian writer and poet, 26, 29, *143*
de la Motte, Diether, *xiv & n*
"Adornos musikalische Analysen," *xiv & n*
Munich, *143*
Musik, Die, x
Musikblätter des Anbruch, see *Anbruch*

National Socialism, 9, 31–32, 72n
neoclassical, neoclassicism, *xiv*, 51, 87, 119, 121, *139*
neudeutsch, 24, 79, 104, 119
Neue deutsche Beiträge, literary journal edited by Hugo von Hofmannsthal, 27, *143*
new objectivity (*Neue Sachlichkeit*), *xiv*, 8, 19, *139*
Nietzsche, Friedrich (1844–1900), *141*
Nuremberg, 13

Österreichische Gesellschaft für Musik, 136
Österreichische Nationalbibliothek, *see* Austrian National Library
Offenbach, Jacques, 131
Olympia, 131
Ossiachersee, lake in Carinthia, Austria, *144*
ostinato, 64, 67, 70, 71, 81, 124

Palestrina, Giovanni da, 32
Paris, 12, 16, *139*
passacaglia, 64, 67, 76, 125
Perle, George, *xvi*, 140
Pfitzner, Hans (1869–1949), German composer; his 1919 polemic against the German critic Paul Bekker led Berg to write a response published in *Anbruch*, 24, 28
Piccaver, Alfred (1884–1958), Austrian tenor; sang at the Vienna Opera 1912–1937, 12
Ploderer, Rudolf (d. 1933), Austrian lawyer; friend of Berg, 29
Poe, Edgar Allen, 117
Prague, 13
Proust, Marcel (1871–1922), French novelist, 12, 21, 27, 34, 63, 114, *142*

Racine, Jean Baptiste, 113n
Raimund, Ferdinand (1790–1836), Austrian actor and playwright, 2
Das Mädchen aus der Feenwelt oder der Bauer als Millionär, 2
Der Verschwender, 2; Valentin, 2
Rathaus, Karol (1895–1954), Polish-American composer; student of Schreker, 29
Ravel, Maurice (1875–1937), 12, 122
Daphnis et Chloë, 122
Redlich, Hans Ferdinand (1903–1968), Austrian-British musicologist; biographer of Berg, xvii, xviii, 95, *138*
"Der grosse Einsame," xvii, *138*
Alban Berg: Versuch einer Würdigung, *138*
Reger, Max (1873–1916), German composer, 3, 28, 54

Index

Reich, Willi (1898–1980), Austrian-
Swiss musicologist; student of
Berg, *xi & n, xiii*, xvii, 9, 16, 28,
37, 135, 136, *138, 140, 143*
Alban Berg, xiii, xvii, 9, 37, 62,
136, *138*
Reinhart, Hans (1880–1963), Swiss
arts patron; brother of Werner
Reinhart, *144*
Reinhart, Werner (1884–1951), Swiss
conductor; brother of Hans
Reinhart, *144*
Rennert, Günther, German stage
director, 129
Rilke, Rainer Maria (1875–1926),
German poet, 50
Rogge, Wolfgang, *143*
ed., *Theodor W. Adorno und Ernst
Krenek Briefwechsel, 143*
Romanticism (also neoromanticism),
47, 48, 50, 51, 52, 75, 76, 85,
118, 119, 121
rondo forms, 7, 36, 54, 55, 59–61,
71, 75, 83, 95, 96, 100, 103, 106,
107, 108–109, 111, 124, 126
Ronsard, Pierre de, 24, *142*
Rottweiler, Hektor (T. W. Adorno
pseudonym), 136, 137
row, row forms, row technique, *xii*,
14, 57, 59, 60, 64, 65, 66, 70, 77,
87, 95, 99, 101–102, 106–107,
110, 134; *see also* twelve-tone
Rudolf Hospital, Vienna, 9

Salzburg Festival, 27
San Martino, town in Italian
Dolomites, 18
Santa Margherita, Italian resort near
Genoa, 26
Satie, Erik (1866–1925), French
composer, 74
Cinq grimaces, 74
Scheler, Max (1874–1928), German
philosopher and sociologist, 23,
142
Schenker, Heinrich (1868–1935),
Austrian music theorist, 36–37
Scherchen, Hermann (1891–1966),
German conductor, 13, 133
scherzo form, 6, 71, 88, 89, 99, 106,
110, 112, 116, 118

Schloss, Julius (1902–1972), student
of Berg, *141*
Schloss Restaurant, Berlin, 13, *141*
Schoenberg, Arnold (1874–1951),
Austrian-American composer;
teacher of Berg and Webern, *viii,
ix, x, xi, xii, xiii, xv, xvi*, xvii,
3, 4, 5, 7, 8, 11–12, 13, 15, 18,
19, 20, 21, 22–23, 25, 27–29,
31, 32, 33, 35, 36, 37–38, 40–42,
48, 49, 50, 53, 63, 64, 66–68,
70–71, 72n, 75–76, 81, 82, 87,
89, 91–93, 94, 95, 96, 99, 102,
103, 105, 106, 112, 121, 122, 126,
127, 129, 133–134, *138, 140, 143*
WORKS (chronologically ordered):
Gurrelieder, 35
Pelleas und Melisande, Op. 5, 35
Eight Songs, Op. 6, *xiii*
String Quartet in D minor, Op. 7,
23, 35, 40, 82
Chamber Symphony No. 1, Op. 9,
23, 35, 36, 40–42, 46, 50, 81
String Quartet in F # minor, Op. 10,
viii, 53, 105, 110, 129; "Litanei,"
105, 110; "Entrückung," *viii*,
112
Fifteen Songs from *Das Buch der
hängenden Gärten* (George),
Op. 15, 33, 66
Five Pieces for Orchestra, Op. 16,
22, 64, 122
Erwartung, Op. 17, 23, 49, 77, 122
Six Little Piano Pieces, Op. 19,
67–68, 70–71, 76; No. 2, 70;
No. 4, 71
Herzgewächse, Op. 20, 48
Pierrot lunaire, Op. 21, 23, 33, 64,
73, 76, 89–91, 129; "Mond-
fleck," 76; "Enthauptung,"
89–91
Die glückliche Hand, Op. 18, 10,
23, 73, 75–76
Die Jakobsleiter, 21
Serenade, Op. 24, 29, 89; March,
29
Wind Quintet, Op. 26, 91, 99
Variations for Orchestra, Op. 31,
122
Von heute auf morgen, Op. 32, 126
Moses and Aron, 133

153

Index

Index

Index